SPINNIN' THE WEBB

CHICK WEBB

THE LITTLE GIANT

by Chet Falzerano

foreword by Van Alexander

edited by Judith Falzerano, Brooks Tegler, and Paul Testa

layout and production by Jim Filippi

ISBN 978-1-57424-309-3

Published by Centerstream Publishing LLC
P. O. Box 17878
Anaheim Hills, CA 92817
Email: centerstrm@aol.com web site: centerstream-usa.com

For my wife and best friend Judith

CONTENTS

INTRODUCTION

My introduction to Chick Webb came in 1976, before I became interested in drum history. Gene Palma, as some of you may know, appeared in Martin Scorsese's box office hit *Taxi Driver* as a street performer demonstrating the drumming technique of Gene Krupa and Chick Webb. At the time I had drummed for 23 years and was of course keenly aware of the iconic Krupa, but also made a curious mental note of Palma's portrayal of Webb.

As I became interested in the history of drums and drummers, that image was refreshed when I acquired a 1939 Gretsch drum catalogue with Chick Webb pictured on the cover…that same upward gaze, arms flailing with mocked enthusiasm. I soon learned it was anything but fake. Webb's command of the drum set was heralded from every historical source consistently with the comment "Recordings do not adequately represent what this guy had to offer." When my drum heroes spoke of him in this manner I naturally became curious. As I gathered information, I soon learned that Webb achieved his reputation in a short albeit fruitful career. Also fascinated with his flair for innovative drum equipment, with the help of my wife Judith I decided to replicate a tribute Chick Webb drum set. Judith then set me on an enjoyable path when she asked, "Why don't you write a book about him?"

Our effort was confirmed when bandleader, composer, arranger, writer, conductor, Van Alexander agreed to write the foreword. For the uninitiated, Alexander has done it all in the music biz. Besides winning several Emmy Awards for his television scores and presented with the Henry Mancini Award for Lifetime Achievement from ASCAP, he has rubbed elbows with the greats of the entertainment industry: Bob Crosby, Benny Goodman, Dinah Shore, Doris Day, Mickey Rooney, Dean Martin, Peggy Lee, James Stewart, Gordon MacRae, Ella Fitzgerald, and of course, Chick Webb.

This tribute to Chick Webb could not have been realized without the help of some special people. My heartfelt thanks to the following for their most needed assistance: Van Alexander, Dave Brown, Harry Cangany, Jon Cohan, Judith Falzerano, Jim Filippi, Mike Kaskell, Ron Middlebrook, Mosaic Records, Brooks Tegler, and Paul Testa.

FOREWORD

When Chet asked me to write the foreword to his book I was a bit reluctant as I had never written an introduction or a foreword to any book, but then my brain started to review sort of a re-run from that wonderful era; I just had to adjust my rear view mirror. I was back, wearing my saddle shoes and listening to all the great bands that played at the legendary Savoy Ballroom in Harlem.

VAN ALEXANDER, AGE 97, AT THE 2013 AMERICAN SOCIETY OF MUSIC ARRANGERS AND COMPOSERS, STUDIO CITY, CA.

It was a cold night in February 1936 when, with fear and trepidation, I approached Chick Webb with whom I had a nodding acquaintance. I asked him if he'd be interested in listening to a couple of my arrangements that I thought would fit his band and style. I was thrilled when he said "Yes." But then I was scared, because I was bluffing. I didn't have any arrangements. I hastened home, got to work, and about ten days later brought two charts (all parts copied out) down to Chick's rehearsal. Let's cut to the chase. He and the guys in the band liked what I did, and I had my first sale ($10 each). I also had my first boss, and the "jump-start" for what turned out to be a great ride for me in the music business.

Ella Fitzgerald had just joined the band, and I was asked to write most of the charts for her early Decca Records. Here I was at age twenty, able to obtain hands-on lessons and to learn and hone my skills on the job. How great was that? Besides our musical association, Chick Webb and I became friends. I spent many enjoyable evenings with him and his lovely wife Sally. The topic of course was always music, arrangements, and how to continually improve his band. The band was his life and he would spend every dime he could muster to buy new arrangements. He hired other arrangers besides myself. There was the great Edgar Sampson (nicknamed "the lamb" because he was such a mild-mannered gentle man). Then from the saxophone section, there was Wayman Carver, and an outsider Charlie Dixon. A few years earlier, Benny Carter did a few charts for the band. Sadly, as far as I know, there are only three of us left who had worked and played at the great Savoy Ballroom and they are Gerald Wilson, Joe Wilder (ed note, Wilder died one month prior to Alexander writing this foreword), and myself.

There have been a few (very few) uninformed critics or would-be musicologists who said derogatory things about Chick Webb...that he lacked compassion, was a tyrant who had a short fuse, etc. etc. Well, I'm here to tell you, nothing is further from the truth. I'll always remember him as a sweet, gentle man who passed away too early, but left the world with a great legacy of his life and musical accomplishments. This book could be used as a reference guide for musical history buffs, and I salute Chet and Judith for its wholesome approval and for its painstaking, accurate documentation.

Van Alexander Los Angeles, CA 2014

P.S. I'm not sure that there is an after-life, but if there is, I know there will be a grand reunion of Chick, Ella and yours truly.

BATTLE MAD

'I don't think there has been anyone who had a better idea how to put together an orchestra and how to play arrangements than Chick. He kept saying, "I want the best band. I've got to go to the top!"' ***Mario Bauza***

William Henry 'Chick' Webb *b.* February 10, 1909 Baltimore, MD, *d.* June 16, 1939 Baltimore, MD.

William Henry 'Chick' Webb made his bones in the near impossible competitive market of New York City shortly after he arrived in 1924. As the song goes "If I can make it there, I'll make it anywhere." The Big Apple, as it was known then and now, has crushed many a dream, but not Chick's. The "Little Giant" was determined to "make it" and make it he did. Considering the odds he was up against, it is no wonder critics, colleagues, and the community in general, sang his praise.

Webb's challenge to "make it" far outreached the convoluted obstacles of New York's capricious expectations of artists, a looming Great Depression, or even racial prejudice, so prevalent at the time. Chick had to overcome a physical barrier. A mere four feet one inch tall, his short stature was a result of him falling down a flight of steps when he was an infant in his East Baltimore family home. Rushed to Johns Hopkins Hospital, it was determined several vertebrae were crushed and surgery was performed. After the surgery Webb never gained full mobility. His malady progressed to tuberculosis of the spine, giving him the appearance of a hunchback and a life of pain. Because of his small, contorted appearance, playmates nicknamed him "Chick." The family doctor suggested he play drums to improve his upper body strength. This advice proved to be a godsend for young Chick. The Webb family was large with not a lot of money to go around. Buying a drum, let alone a set of drums, was out of the question. Even drumsticks were not within the family budget. Undaunted, Chick made his own drumsticks and the world became his drum. Not just the usual kitchen pots and pans most drummers start with, but any flat surface. Garbage cans, sidewalks, marble stoops, iron porch railings, lampposts, anything was subject to his relentless percussion attacks. Webb's friends no longer saw him as the funny looking little "Chick," but "drum-mad."[1] Chick grew to appreciate this admiration replacing ridicule from his playmates. "Trick drumming came naturally to him and passers-by rewarded him generously when he performed on the streets."[2] Also accepting every odd job Chick could find, he saved for a professional set of drums. He claimed he could sell up to 4,000 newspapers per day (but probably it was more like 400). Finally accumulating $103, at age eleven, he bought his first albeit used drum set. "Before long he had a semi-steady job (playing drums) on one of the excursion boats which crossed back and forth on Sheepshead Bay. On Saturday nights he would make as much as fifteen dollars, which seemed a fortune to an eleven year old boy. The first steady band Webb ever worked with was the Jazzola Band (on one of the segregated excursion boats), and there Chick formed a life long friendship"[3] with guitarist John Trueheart. Local success came easily for the pair and with a little savings and a lot of confidence, in 1924, they decided to try their hand in New York's "Big Apple." When they arrived in Harlem, Chick was a mere 15 years old, Trueheart three years his senior.

SMALL'S PARADISE, HARLEM, NEW YORK

Webb and Trueheart held up in a one-room cold water flat, taking every opportunity to meet with other aspiring musicians especially at the legendary all-night jam sessions. "Big-time, established players need proof that the new kid deserves to be in their company. That proof came in jam sessions, generally held after hours in clubs or apartments uptown."[4] Paramount among those were the Sunday jam sessions at the newly opened (1925) Small's Paradise in Harlem. There, Webb formed associations with Johnny Hodges, Benny Carter and Duke Ellington. It was his friendship with Bobby Stark that led to his first gig. Stark was playing trumpet in Edgar Dowell's Band and asked Webb to tag along when

[1] No author credited, "The Rise of a Crippled Genius," *Down Beat*, December 1937.

[2] Burt Korall, *Drummin' Men* (New York: Schirmer Books, 1990).

[3] No author credited, "The Rise of a Crippled Genius," *Down Beat*, December 1937.

[4] Burt Korall, *Drummin' Men* (New York: Schirmer Books, 1990).

Dowell arranged an audition for his band in a club uptown. Dowell's regular drummer got lost in the subway and Stark persuaded Dowell to let Chick fill in the position. Though dubious of what he saw of Chick, Dowell did not want to lose the audition and agreed. Very often, Chick's physical appearance prevented him from even being considered for an audition. But Webb's performance was so dynamic, the club owner hired the band with the requirement that Chick be the featured drummer. Word got around quickly that little Chick Webb was a drummer to be reckoned with. Other musicians would spend their free evenings checking out this little dynamo when he played one-nighters with pick-up bands.

In 1926, Webb was offered his first job as a bandleader. Duke Ellington was working at the Kentucky Club when he got word that the Black Bottom Club needed a band. As Chick Webb's most outspoken admirer he proposed that Webb form a band and Ellington would persuade the Black Bottom owners to book the new band. Webb wanted no part of it. "'At that time,' Ellington explained in *Hear Me Talkin' to Ya*, 'Chick wasn't thinking anything about getting along on his own, his mind was all on the drums.'"[5] It was Johnny Hodges, Chick's first cousin, who talked the stubborn Webb into formulating a five-piece group, one of the first bands with a drummer as a leader (Ben Pollack was one year earlier). Members of the group, named the "Harlem Stompers," were Hodges on alto, Bobby Stark/trumpet, pianist Don Kirkpatrick, Trueheart/guitar, and Chick holding down the positions of drums and leader. The gig paid an astonishing $200 a week ($30 of which went to Ellington as a commission) and lasted five months. Ellington then booked the Webb orchestra at the Paddock Club on 50th Street. Chick expanded the group to eight members by adding Elmer Williams on tenor, a trombonist known as "Slats," and an unnamed bass player. Unfortunately, the Paddock was destroyed in a fire later that year and the Harlem Stompers found themselves out of work. In 1927 Webb signed a contract with the Savoy Ballroom.

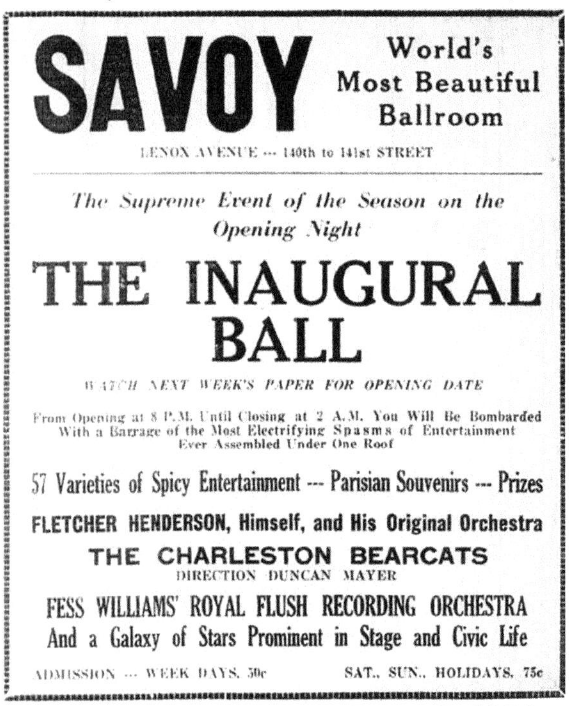

New York Amsterdam News, March 3, 1926

The Savoy announced its Inaugural Ball for Friday March 12, 1926 with advertisements boasting "The Supreme Event of the Season Opening at 8 PM Until Closing at 2AM You Will Be Bombarded With a Barrage of the Most Electrifying Spasms of Entertainment Ever Assembled Under One Roof. 57 Varieties of Spicy Entertainment-Parisian Souvenirs-Prizes" The next day the *New York Age* newspaper covered the event with "**Savoy Turns 2,000 Away On Opening Night – Crowds Pack Ballroom All Week** So great was the throng that tried to attend the inaugural ball of the new Savoy ballroom Friday night March 12 a squad of police from the 16th Precinct ordered the doors closed at twelve o'clock and refused to allow any more tickets to be sold. Between midnight and 1 o'clock it was estimated that no less than 2,000 people sought to enter the building. Those who were fortunate to get inside, witnessed an interesting vaudeville program and enjoyed the dancing to the strains of music furnished by three orchestras."[6] While the seventeen year old Webb was experiencing his first gig as a bandleader at the Black Bottom, he surely was keeping a keen eye on the three bands booked that night at the Savoy: Fletcher Henderson and the Roseland Orchestra, The Charleston Bearcats, and Fess Williams' Royal Flush Orchestra. Webb's life challenges were after all, a stacked deck against him up to this point. He systematically overcame those challenges to

[5] Contemporary Musicians, edited by Michael L LaBlanc, et al, The Gale Group, "Gale Musicians Profile: Chick Webb," http://www.answers.com/topic/chick-webb

[6] No author credited, "Savoy Turns 2,000 Away On Opening Night – Crowds Pack Ballroom All Week," *New York Age*, March 20, 1926.

become a preeminent drummer at an early age. Ellington understood Webb's reluctance to take on the role of bandleader, preferring to advance his drumming skills. Notwithstanding, Webb accepted the additional challenge and during this period he certainly scrutinized his new peers. "Mario Bauza, 'I don't think there has been anyone who had a better idea how to put together an orchestra and how to play arrangements than Chick. He kept saying, "I want the best band. I've got to go to the top!""'"[7]

The Savoy, located in the middle of Harlem on Lenox Avenue, ran the entire block between 140th and 141st Street, and was the brainchild of Moe Gale (Moses Gailwski). He recruited two other financial partners, his cousin Charles Gailwski, and Charles Buchanan, who also served as the ballroom's manager. Buchanan had a staff of 90, including administrative assistants, waiters, porters, hostesses, cashiers, and a team of tuxedo-clad bouncers. The ballroom was located on the second floor with a grand entrance located in the middle of the block on the first floor. The marquee that spanned the entire sidewalk proclaimed "Savoy World's Finest Ballroom." The lobby featured a cut glass chandelier and marble steps leading to the grand ballroom. Measuring a spacious 200 feet by 50 feet, the wood dance floor included a suspension system to accommodate up to 4,000 pulsating patrons. Because of its constant use, it needed to be replaced every three years. The mirrored walls not only gave the impression of even a larger room, but also the opportunity for dancers to view their choreography and that of their contemporaries as well. Unlike most other ballrooms in Harlem, Moe Gale had the good sense to open his doors to everyone. His pricey Cotton Club neighbor on the next block strictly enforced a "whites only" patron policy. Gale instinctively knew a non-segregated nightspot in the middle of Harlem would be a success…and it was. "It is estimated that the ballroom generated $250,000 in annual profit in its peak years. Each year, the ballroom was visited by near 700,000 people. The normal entrance fee was 30 to 85 cents per person, depending on what time a person came. 30 cents was the base price, but after 6pm the fee was 60 cents, and then 85 cents after 8pm."[8] Clientele included the famous and not so famous. The occasional "surprise guest" like Clark Gable, Mickey Rooney, Orson Welles, Greta Garbo, Judy Garland, Fred Astaire and Lana Turner made the Savoy the place to see and be seen. In fact, it was Lana Turner who inspired the nickname "The home of happy feet" when she made the comment, "What happy feet these people have."

SAVOY BALLROOM, HARLEM, NEW YORK

More importantly, it was a respectable place. Order was maintained by well-clad but robust bouncers and unlike the Cotton Club, whose doors police closed on several occasions for ignoring prohibition (1920-1933), the Savoy had a strict no-alcohol policy. "Only soft drinks are served and the average price of drinks are only from 15 to 50 cents. This means that one can go to the place and enjoy a most pleasant evening under the best auspices without having to pay the exorbitant charges which have been the case in the cabarets here for years. There has been no extra charge for dancers…a slight charge is made only when individuals desiring to dance with professional instructresses are asked to pay a small fee. Those entering with their own

[7] Burt Korall, *Drummin' Men* (New York: Schirmer Books, 1990).

[8] No author credited, "Savoy Ballroom," http://en.wikipedia.org/wiki/Savoy_Ballroom

ladies or their own escorts can dance without any extra charge."[9] This safe, inexpensive environment drew young single women by the throngs, which in turn, drew their suitors, all for the sole purpose of having a good time...and to dance, dance, dance.

SAVOY LINDY HOPPERS ("SHORTY" GEORGE SNOWDEN, LEFT)

To facilitate this, the ballroom was designed with two bandstands along the east wall of the Savoy. As one band finished their set, another immediately started. Music therefore, was non-stop and so was the dancing. This multiple band set-up was good news for local musicians looking for venues to fill their schedules. Charles Buchanan's managerial responsibilities included hiring bands for the Savoy and he did it laudably. Fortunately for Webb, that included hiring the Harlem Stompers as the house band in 1927. Either Buchanan, or the shrewd businessman Moe Gale noticed that as one band finished their set, the next band tried to one-up their predecessor. The Savoy's nickname in the neighborhood was "The Track" because of its elongated dance floor and competitive dance environment. The musicians seemed to be included in this infectious competition as well. To feed this frenzy, someone came up with the idea of having a battle of the bands. On May 15, 1927 Buchanan booked four bands for an evening billed as the "Battle of Jazz." Heading the bill was King Oliver's Dixie Syncopators with Paul Barbarin on drums, then Fletcher Henderson and the Roseland Orchestra with Kaiser Marshall on drums, followed by Fess Williams and His Royal Flush Orchestra with Ralph Bedell on drums, and a relatively unknown house band, Chick Webb and his Harlem Stompers. While Chick was only eighteen years old at the time, Joe "King" Oliver had an impressive seventeen year's experience as a jazz musician dating back to New Orleans "Storyville" days. Fletcher Henderson was also a formidable contender working with the likes of Louis Armstrong and Coleman Hawkins. He was a prolific recording artist, credited with 80 individual sides in 1924 alone (remember this was before albums when records were

KING OLIVER DIXIE SYNCOPATORS, FLETCHER HENDERSON AND THE ROSELAND ORCHESTRA, FESS WILLIAMS AND HIS ROYAL FLUSH ORCHESTRA

issued on 2-sided 78rpm discs). Fess Williams, though not as popular, was a favorite along with Henderson at the Savoy, both were featured opening night one year earlier. One would think little Chick would enter this foray somewhat intimidated. With less than one year of intense preparation as a leader of his new band, he entered the arena like David and the Goliath, defeating all three giants. "The Webb crew won hands

[9] No author credited, "Thousands Storm New Savoy at Big Opening, Mar. 12," *New York Amsterdam News*, March 17, 1926.

down. Moving through imaginative 'head' arrangements - these were worked out by members of the band, memorized, and seldom written down - with enviable elan and pulsation, Webb and his family of players became the talk of Harlem."[10] One particular arrangement was heralded by *Down Beat* magazine, reporting on the night's events. "They (King Oliver) had one number which was definitely conceded to be a 'Killer.' It was called 'Cat.' It so happened that Chick and the boys had their own arrangement of this number and after they had got through playing it, Oliver never took it out of his books again, as long as he stayed at the Savoy. Paul Barbarin was drumming with Oliver at the time and was recognized as top man. When they opened, he had not bothered to even speak to Chick, so confident was he, but when they had finished out the evening, he came over to Webb with an apology."[11]

So what was it that Chick Webb and the Harlem Stompers did that night to overwhelmingly out-master three of the current giants of jazz? "Paul Barbarin was a New Orleans jazz drummer, usually regarded (along with Baby Dodds) as one of the very best pre-Big Band era jazz drummers"[12] and yet he humbly offered his hand in apology to Chick at the end of the evening. Why? Webb was an innovator. "Webb had little room in his life for anything but music. 'Music comes first,' he often declared. When he wasn't playing, he thought and talked about music and how it should be played. He constantly mulled over the drummer's role in a band and what could be done to make the drummer more of a contributing factor in the music he loved."[13] At the tender age of 18, when most lads are headstrong and full of ambition, Webb realized his dream of getting "to the top" required meaningful collaboration within his ensemble. The Harlem Stompers obviously thought as one and along with some of their contemporaries, were experimenting with a new musical style later to be known as "swing." It is generally regarded that the musical genre "swing" was birthed by Duke Ellington's 1931 composition "It Don't Mean A Thing If It Ain't Got That Swing." Indeed, that was the first time "swing" occurred in a title of a composition, but its origins were earlier. "The styles of jazz that were popular from the teens through the late 1920's were usually played with rhythms with a two beat feel, and often attempted to reproduce the style of contrapuntal improvisation developed by the first generation of jazz musicians in New Orleans. In the 1920's, a subtle stylistic shift took place in the rhythm, which developed a four beat feel with a smoothly syncopated style of playing the melody, while the rhythm section supported it with a steady four to the bar. (Louis Armstrong got to the heart of the matter) during a nationwide broadcast of the Bing Crosby (radio) Show. Crosby said 'We have as our guest the master of swing and I'm going to get him to tell you what swing music is.' Armstrong said, 'Ah, swing, well, we used to call it syncopation – then they called it ragtime, then blues – then jazz. Now it's swing. White folks, yo' all sho is a mess.'"[14] Transitions in music, as with all art, cannot be pinpointed. The seeds were being sowed.

ROSE DANCELAND, HARLEM, NEW YORK

"After his contract expired at the Savoy, Webb booked his band at the Rose Danceland on 125th Street in December of 1927. Instead of staying at the Rose Danceland, however, Webb took a job playing behind vaudeville dancers. Ill-suited for

[10] Burt Korall, *Drummin' Men* (New York: Schirmer Books, 1990).
[11] No author credited, "The Rise of a Crippled Genius," *Down Beat*, December 1937.
[12] No author credited, "Paul Barbarin," http://en.wikipedia.org/wiki/Paul_Barbarin
[13] Burt Korall, *Drummin' Men* (New York: Schirmer Books, 1990).
[14] No author credited, "Swing Music 1920s: Origins," http://en.wikipedia.org/wiki/Swing_music

ROSELAND, HARLEM, NEW YORK

the engagement, the band not only lost the job, but outraged the owners of the Rose Danceland, who became embittered at the financial loss incurred by Webb's sudden departure. The lack of steady work and the erratic management by Webb forced several musicians to leave the band. Among them were key soloists like Hodges, who joined Ellington, and Stark, who periodically left for employment with Fletcher Henderson."[15] Webb was quick to learn the ropes as a musician, then bandleader, but his business skills needed work. Moreover, in a segregated marketplace, whites controlled business. A black band without white representation resulted in rough times and the band had lapses between sporadic engagements. Those included Roseland, the Cotton Club, the Strand Roof, and the Savoy, with the next battle of the bands on May 6, 1928. Billed as "Jazzwar," Charles Buchanan hired an additional four lesser-known bands to battle with Chick: Drummer/Bandleader Lloyd Scott and His Symphonic Syncopators, Alex Jackson's Plantation Orchestra with Dick Ward on drums, Charlie Johnson's Paradise Orchestra with George Stafford on drums, and once again, Fess Williams and His Royal Flush Orchestra with Ralph Bedell on drums. Even with Webb's band members in a state of flux, it was a bloodbath. In his book *Drummin' Men*, Burt Korall quotes Allen Paley, "The man (Webb) was one of a kind. There won't be another like him again. I've heard an awful lot of drummers. But he was the best natural player I ever came across. Fast, clean, flawless, he played like a machine gun…but with enormous feeling and understanding of what the band was trying to do. It was almost barbaric the way he drove that band. He'd break things up, developing ideas off the cow bell, the cymbals, the tom-toms, using the snare drum as his basic instrument. It would get so disjointed many of us would shake our heads, knowing we could never fully unravel what he played. But for all their 'mystery,' his performances had logic to them"[16] The best recorded example of this is "Sing Me A Swing Song" where Chick executes a wildly mixed up sixteenth note cowbell/snare/woodblock break in shout chorus, while Ella sings "Old Chick Webb is beatin' it out."

COTTON CLUB, HARLEM, NEW YORK

Little is known about Webb's equipment during this period. Allen Paley continues, "He'd hold the sticks - 7A's, very thin - by the butt and use them just like whips."[17] For a kid who couldn't even afford a pair of drumsticks a few years earlier, visiting New York's "Music Row" (48th Street off Times Square) must have been a revelation. One music store in particular, Frank Wolf Drummers Supplies, offered an item that immediately caught Chick's eye, the Billy Gladstone Hand Sock Cymbals. Billy Gladstone was a percussionist at the Capitol Theatre on Broadway in New York City. "Gladstone's command of snare drum technique was not his only claim to fame. He was also a consummate inventor with more that 20 US patents credited

FRANK WOLF DRUMMERS SUPPLIES, TIMES SQUARE, NEW YORK CITY

[15] Contemporary Musicians, edited by Michael L LaBlanc, et al, The Gale Group, "Gale Musicians Profile: Chick Webb," http://www.answers.com/topic/chick-webb
[16] Burt Korall, *Drummin' Men* (New York: Schirmer Books, 1990).
[17] Ibid.

to him."[18] Gladstone was the inventor of the Hand Sock; Frank Wolf was the manufacturer and offered it in his store. Listed in the 1927 Leedy Drum Catalogue, the description reads, "They consist of two deep cup brass cymbals, operated by hand-grip aluminum scissors. The cymbals are permanently attached and strike together flat, producing the very 'sock' effect desired. A world of varied effects can be obtained. Will either 'sock' or ring. Wonderful for flash work. Many drummers use them for solo work."[19]

BILLY GLADSTONE LEFT. FRANK WOLF (DEMONSTRATING HAND SOCK) TO HIS RIGHT

Indeed, Webb used this unique instrument in his first record release "Dog Bottom" (Brunswick Records, 799 7th Avenue, New York City) June 14, 1929. Curiously, the label does not reference the "Harlem Stompers," but instead "The Jungle Band." Webb may have been busy finding replacements for departing musicians from his stage band during this lean period, but for this first recording session the personnel were: Ward Pinkett (tp, vo), Edwin Swayzee (tp), Robert Horton (tb), Hilton Jefferson, Louis Jordan (as), Elmer Williams (ts), Don Kirkpatrick (p), John Trueheart (bjo), Elmer James (tu), Chick Webb (d). Webb's "drums" consisted only of the "Hand Sock," probably to the relief of the recording engineer at the session. In those days, recording equipment supposedly could not cope with drums. Very often drummers were not allowed to use a bass drum in the studio. The unobtrusive Hand Sock was greeted with open arms. Webb also used the Hand Sock in a later recording of "I Got Rhythm." Interesting in the "Dog Bottom" recording that Pinkett's vocals were "scat," an idiom supposedly introduced by Louis Armstrong in his recording "Heebie Jeebies" one year earlier. Note the transition from the earlier New Orleans' two beat feel to a more swinging feel of four, not Swing, but certainly not Dixieland either.

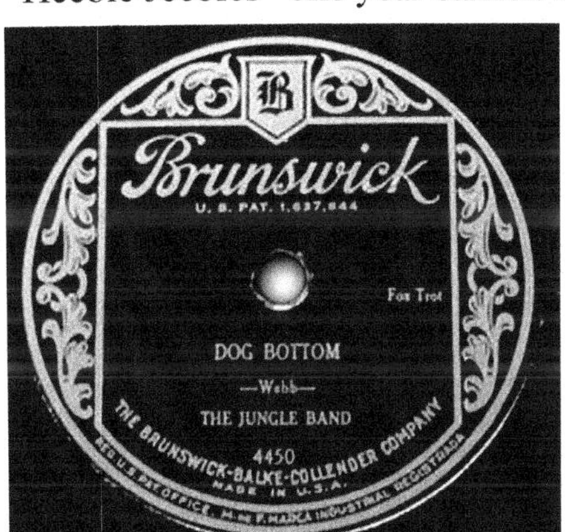

"DOG BOTTOM" BRUNSWICK RECORDS, 1929

Two weeks later (June 27) the "B" side "Jungle Mama" was recorded with the same personnel but with the reeds doubling on clarinet and Trueheart on guitar. These sessions were not the first for Webb. Two years earlier (August 25, 1927), Webb and the Harlem Stompers entered the Vocalion Studios, New York City to record "Low Levee – High Water." Unfortunately, it was never released and the masters no longer exist.

CHICK SOLOING WITH THE HAND SOCK

Also in 1929, Webb and his Harlem Stompers appeared in a Kukor/Lasky 15 minute film short *After Seben*, with James Barton. In the film, Barton, a white Vaudeville comic, performs in "black face" as the emcee and solo dancer at a Harlem nightspot. At 07:55 we see

[18] Chet Falzerano, *Billy Gladstone* (Fullerton, CA: Centerstream Publishing, 2007).

[19] No author credited, *Leedy Topics* (Leedy Drum Publications, April 1927).

a few seconds of Webb surrounded by his Harlem Stompers. His abbreviated set consists of a snare drum, a Chinese tom, Chinese cymbal, and what appears to be a 28 inch bass drum decorated with a country scene painted on the front head. As the band begins to play "Sweet Sue," Chick joins in on snare drum. Unfortunately the film's sound quality does not offer much to reveal Webb's playing save a few snare accents. His records, because of the limitations of recording equipment during this period, also lack true insight. Van

CHICK WEBB (RIGHT, HOLDING HAND SOCK) AND THE HARLEM STOMPERS

Alexander, "The records keep Chick's enormous talent a secret. They only suggest what he could do. I saw and heard him live night after night and it was never less than exhilarating. He felt such happiness when he played and transmitted a spark to the players. The man was inspiring."[20] Burt Korall, "What drummers like Gene Krupa, Allen Paley, Buddy Rich, Johnny Blowers, and Jim Chapin, among others, heard at the Savoy is best described as 'otherworldly.' 'Even on records,' Chapin says, 'you're not sure what he played. The accents are so various; there's so much.'"[21]

HOT CHOCOLATES REVIEW

Sometime during 1930, Webb and the Harlem Stompers toured with the "Hot Chocolates Review," however as of this writing, no details are known. Battle of the bands continued at the Savoy on May 14, 1930. This time Charles Buchanan upped the ante on Webb, booking Webb's old pal Duke Ellington and His Orchestra with Sonny Greer on drums, Cab Calloway and the Missourians with Leroy Maxey as his drummer, plus lesser known Cecil Scott and his Bright Boys with Arnold Bolden on drums, and Lockwood Lewis Orchestra with an unknown drummer. Before one of the Ellington battles started, "Webb spied Sonny Greer setting up and tuning his battery of instruments. He leaned over to (Teddy) McRae and asked, 'What is he tuning up for?

[20] Burt Korall, *Drummin' Men* (New York: Schirmer Books, 1990).

[21] Ibid.

I'm gonna kill him before he gets started.' McRae, 'And he did.'"[22] To some, this may seem an arrogant statement on Chick's part. It wasn't. He knew his job and nothing would stand in his way to complete the task at hand. "Though he had a strong sense of self, Webb was highly receptive to the needs of others. Musicians in and out of the band were given credit and respect for their accomplishments. Drummers he admired such as Ray Bauduc, Krupa, (Jo Jones, Sonny Greer), and Dave Tough, were treated warmly and with deference. Webb didn't bad-mouth people. He was optimistic and had an engaging flair for the humorous. Webb was totally loyal to his friends and those musically associated with him. He helped trumpeter Cootie Williams, who worked with him and lived with him for a period. The drummer was close to Johnny Hodges. Webb also had a key relationship with Mario Bauza. He brought Bauza into the band and every night after work, he showed the young Cuban musician how to play his music. Few leaders would have done that for a sideman."[23] Everyone loved Chick, especially Ellington, despite the fact that he and his fellow contenders were summarily vanquished by Webb that night. Ellington understood Chick probably better than anyone else, though once referring to him as "Battle Mad." By all accounts, Duke was Chick's best friend, save only for, aptly named, John Trueheart. Separated only by illness, they remained together since the Jazzola gig in Baltimore.

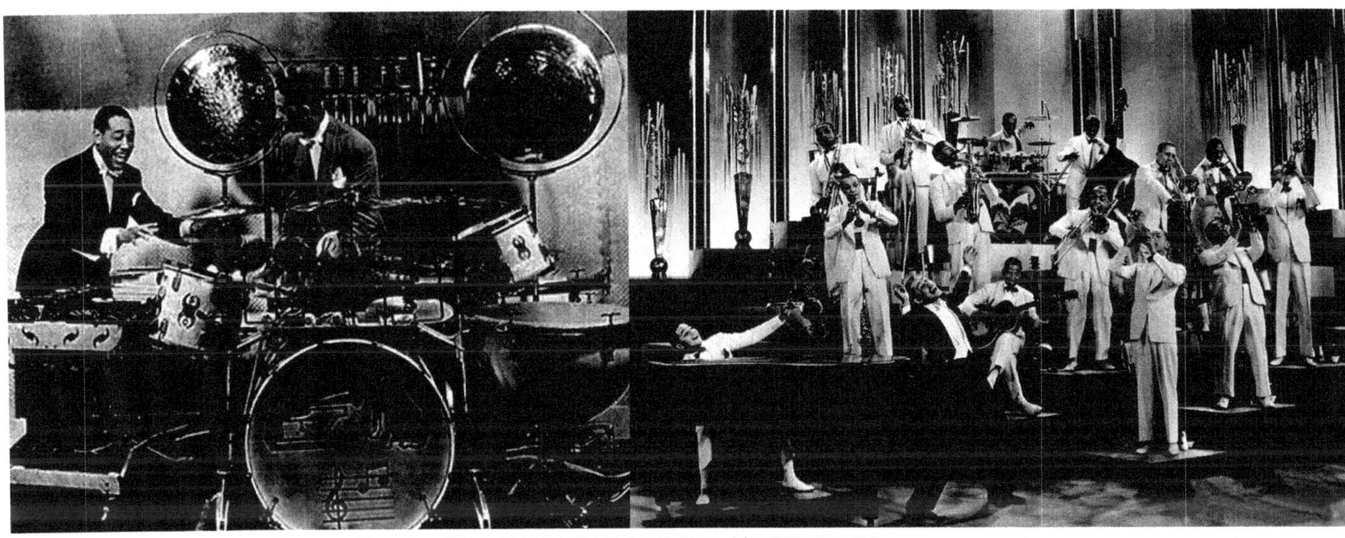

DUKE ELLINGTON WITH SONNY GREER, CAB CALLOWAY AND THE MISSOURIANS

[22] Ibid.
[23] Ibid.

Chick Webb and Duke Ellington with Artie Shaw looking on.

DAWN OF SWING

"I found direction when I first heard Chick. He changed everything around for me, not long after I came to New York. Why? He thought in an original way and knew exactly what to do, particularly in a big band. All of us in that 'learnin' groove' in the 1930's were enlightened by him.' **Gene Krupa**

The man admiring Webb and Ellington's intimate mugging for the camera on the previous page is Artie Shaw. A native New Yorker, Shaw took up the clarinet at age 16 after playing saxophone. Touring with several bands he returned to New York drawn by a new genre of jazz spearheaded by stride pianists Duke Ellington, Jelly Roll Morton, Willie "The Lion" Smith, and Fats Waller. Jazz became an integral part of the Harlem Renaissance, a new culture, known at the time as the "New Negro Movement." Outside Harlem, most white musicians were performing unemotional "society music." When they wanted to stretch their new "jazz legs," they frequented Harlem after-hours spots to study and sit-in with the likes of Louis Armstrong, Fletcher Henderson, Sidney Bechet, and Duke Ellington. Artie Shaw," In 1929, not long after I arrived in New York, I found my way to Harlem. I was just a kid – nineteen years old. Because I was a reader even then and excited by writers who spoke of Harlem (Renaissance) in their books and articles, it seemed the place to go and get to know. One night – I was walking up Lenox, near 140th Street, on my way to Pod and Jerry's to play with Willie "The Lion" Smith. I heard this band really blowing! What a surprise! There were no bands around town like that. The only band that came close in that period was the one led by Fletcher Henderson. As I moved into the Savoy Ballroom, the music hit me head on. It didn't take me long to find out it was Chick Webb's band. I selected a spot near the drums. And things got even better. God, the sound Chick got out of those drums. What he did almost blew me away. He performed with such power and originality. Unlike most people, Chick realized that drums are a *musical* instrument. He knew that unless drums are treated in a musical way, they're terrible, a burden to other players. He must have *heard* really well because what he played was extremely apropos to what was going on. Besides that, Chick was very forceful, propulsive. He literally lifted that band. When it cut lose, he was behind every phrase like a charioteer driving horses. No question about it. Chick was unique in his day. The guy was a force of nature. He came at you! His bass drum shots at the Savoy – I can feel them vibrating in my upper chest and abdomen right now. Offstage

CHICK WEBB, ARTIE SHAW, AND DUKE ELLINGTON AT A BRUNSWICK RECORDS JAM SESSION. (VAN ALEXANDER, LEFT BACK ROW)

LINDBERGH HOPS OFF FOR PARIS

HOME THE BALTIMORE NEWS EXTRA

DARING FLIER STARTS OCEAN DASH ALONE

ROOSEVELT FLYING FIELD, N. Y., May 20.—Braving the perils of rainstorms and fog over the North Atlantic, Capt. Charles A. Lindbergh, the young daredevil American aviator, hopped off on the 3600-mile non-stop, trans-ocean flight for Paris this morning in his Ryan monoplane, Spirit of St. Louis. Lindbergh took the air at 7.52 o'clock. Flying alone and carrying only sandwiches, a few chocolate bars and some distilled water, Lindbergh departed in misty weather. Rain earlier in the night had ceased at 4 o'clock.

All Aboard! Paris Is the Next Stop!

you would never suspect he could be so highly charged. Chick was a quietly, friendly, affable, thoroughly unpretentious person. Later we became good friends and played together. There was a jam session that's affixed in my memory. Chick, Duke and I got it going."[1] This photo of the jam session was taken at the Brunswick studios in 1937. Among the many notable onlookers is Van Alexander on the far left, back row.

Another consequence of the Harlem Black Renaissance was dance, specifically the Lindy Hop. On May 20, 1927, an obscure US Air Mail pilot soared to world fame when he flew his single-seat, single-engine, monoplane, the *Spirit of St. Louis*, non-stop from Long Island, New York, to Paris, France. As a result, Charles A. Lindbergh was the first man to be in New York at 7:25AM one day and Paris, at 10:22PM the next, an astonishing 3,610 miles. A crowd of 150,000 spectators anxiously awaited his arrival at Le Bourget Airfield near Paris, while millions viewed newspaper headlines, "Lindbergh Hops Off For Paris." Some accounts discredit the naming of the new Lindy Hop dance craze to Lindbergh's historic event, but the coincidence is too great, especially considering the magnitude of public opinion at the time. Lindbergh was a world hero. Like all art, dance is an evolutionary process. Early stages of the Lindy Hop were an extension of the then popular Charleston, the Texas Tommy, and the Breakaway. Both music and dance were evolving simultaneously during this period in Harlem. And it occurred at the Savoy. Musicians and dancers were fiercely competing for their share of the attention. Charles Buchanan hired the newly formed dance troop of *Whitey's Lindy Hoppers*, organized by Herbert White, ex-prizefighter and former head bouncer at the Savoy. The purpose was to entertain guests and inspire the brave to join in, sometimes engaging the veterans of this new dance craze to provide instruction. Other dancers to gain recognition on the Savoy dance floor were Frankie "Musclehead" Manning and "Shorty" George Snowden. This elite group sectioned off a portion of the dance floor, known as "Kat's Corner," where only the best were permitted to show their stuff. New steps were continually developed in an improvised style similar to the improvised jazz music. Webb saw this as an opportunity. "Andy Kirk, 'During an evening, he'd (Webb) get some wonderful things going with the dancers. He could translate into percussive terms what they were doing. He caught everything

WHITEY'S LINDY HOPPERS

FRANKIE "MUSCLEHEAD" MANNING

[1] Ibid.

the dancers did, tricks and all. It was a show in itself. And he'd swing that band! Everything was definite, every accent. The whole band was him, really. Being a sickly little fellow, I don't know where he got the energy. But he played boldly. All his strength was in his music.' Doc Cheatham, 'Chick's band had the right style that suited the dancers at the Savoy. His tempos were right for them – not too fast or too slow. Remember, those lindy hoppers had a lot to do with the bands that succeeded at that place. Who was booked and who stayed on depended on them.' Jervis Anderson, 'Webb's group played what came to be called "the Savoy tempo." Duke Ellington later remarked that Webb's "command of his audiences" sprang from his "communication with the dancers" – and what their feet were doing.'"[2] Knowing he had a good thing going, in 1931 Moe Gale signed the newly named Chick Webb Orchestra to an annual contract that would be renewed for the next 5 years. Some critics claim this was Webb's best band with the likes of Benny Carter, Louis Jordan, Mario Bauza, Don Redman, and of course his pal, John Trueheart. 1931 also saw a return to the Brunswick recording studios to lay down the tracks of "Heebie Jeebies," "I'm Left With The Blues In My Heart," and "Soft And Sweet." Benny Carter was the arranger on all three tracks.

MOE GALE AND CHICK WEBB

LEEDY PAINTED BASS DRUM

Two significant events occurred in 1932. Webb's growing popularity won the attention of the Leedy Drum Company, Elkhart, IN. In their March, 1932 publication *Leedy Topics*, a photo of Webb appears with, "'Have used all makes of drums, I find Leedy the best,' that is the tribute to Leedy of Chick Webb of Baltimore, Md. Mr. Webb has had his own orchestra for five years. In the past he has played at the Roseland Ballroom in N.Y., Cotton Club, N.Y., Savoy Ballroom, N.Y., and 'Nuttings on the Charles', Boston."[3] Although we see Chick holding only a Leedy snare drum in some promotional photos, this endorsement may date back to the *After Seben* film short. Though that drum set cannot be identified because of poor film quality, most drum companies offered a drum set with the same painted country scene on the bass drum head. On December 21, Webb entered the Victor Talking Machine Company in Camden,

LOUIS ARMSTRONG

[2] Ibid.
[3] No author credited, *Leedy Topics* (Leedy Drum Publications, March 1932).

New Jersey to record four cuts with Louis Armstrong, "That's My Home," "Hobo You Can't Ride This Train," "I Hate To Leave You Now," and "You'll Wish You'd Never Been Born." This association, plus an imminent tour with Armstrong, further enhanced Webb's already escalating rise in popularity. Armstrong was already a veteran of the New Orleans, Chicago and New York jazz scenes, starred in two Broadway productions, *Hot Chocolates* and *Ain't Misbehavin'*, and multiple recording sessions. Fortunately, Chick was receiving the respect he richly deserved. While most everyone during this period was suffering the disastrous economic effects of The Great Depression, Webb's fortunes were just beginning. Though he never realized the compensation of his white colleagues, for a black man in troubled times, he did OK. "... because living was reasonable in Harlem, he sent most of his money home to Baltimore." "Webb began to diversify his music in the mid and late 30's. He bought arrangements from a variety of key writers and traded charts with other bands. It was a struggle; he had to make money out of his meager salary. First he used the arrangements of Benny Carter and Don Redman; later he hired Charlie Dixon, Van Alexander, Dick Vance, Kenneth Anderson, and other arrangers to give his band a sense of direction. Composer-arranger Edgar Sampson was crucial in creating an image for the band. His riffy concoctions, well-suited to the band's rhythmic focus, blended the written with the improvised in a natural, often provocative manner. His melodious originals, notably "Stompin' at the Savoy" and "Don't Be That Way," (A Goodman staple that Webb swings up a notch...with brushes!) brought Webb special recognition, but only became Swing Era anthems after Benny Goodman recorded them. Mario Bauza, 'Chick was a musician's bandleader – not exactly a leader who was *that* concerned about the public. He cared more about how *he* thought the music should be played. Sometimes he didn't have room rent because he had to pay arrangers – the top guys.'"[4]

"STOMPIN' AT THE SAVOY"

After two more recording sessions in 1934, one as a sideman with Mezz Mezzrow and his Orchestra, Webb entered the Columbia studios with his orchestra to record "Stompin' At The Savoy," truly a Swing Era anthem. This is the first recording that we hear Chick doing send offs on the snare drum in the shout chorus, albeit very subdued. One can only imagine what he did live on stage, especially at the Savoy. Van Alexander clarifies who wrote "Stompin' At The Savoy." "He (Edgar Sampson) was there before I started with the band," he said. "He was the *true* writer of Stompin' At the Savoy, although it came out written by Edgar Sampson, (with) Benny Goodman, and Chick Webb, who had nothing to do with it, outside of recording it."[5] By then Swing had evolved to a definite four beat feel, established by a pulsating rhythm section. Though Webb's recording of "*Stompin' At The Savoy*" rose to number ten on the charts in 1934, Benny Goodman's version two years later was a bigger hit. Difficult to imagine if you listen to both recordings, as Goodman's version seems comically affected and certainly less swinging by comparison. Part of the Webb orchestra's swinging feel was a result of Webb's newly acquired John Kirby, the bass player Chick recorded with in Mezz Mezzrow's session. Kirby joined the

MAX ON SWING

[4] Burt Korall, *Drummin' Men* (New York: Schirmer Books, 1990).

[5] Christopher Popa "CHICK WEBB 'Stompin' At the Savoy'" (http://www.bigbandlibrary.com/chickwebb.html 2004).

Webb organization after working with Fletcher Henderson, and then left Webb to form his own group. While he was with Webb, he maintained some infectious grooves with Chick and his guitarist, John Trueheart. Webb was not the sole pioneer of this infectious rhythm of swing, though arguably the best (certainly at the Savoy). He had no formal training and could not read music throughout his career. Only one swing drumming book was available during this period, written by British swing drummer Max Bacon. In the foreword to his 1934 *Max On Swing*, Bacon writes," It is no exaggeration to say that there are scores of books published on the subject of drums and drumming. Many of them are useful and of great assistance: some of them are excellent. And they cover between them practically every phase on the subject. I say 'practically every phase,' because – so far as I can discover – there is yet no book available which deals with the work of the modern 'swing' drummer. In the past year or so, the ultra-rhythmic type of 'swing' work has made such rapid forward strides that it has become a style of first importance to every enthusiastic percussionist, be he professional or amateur. So much can be said concerning this fascinating way of handling the rhythm that it cannot be dealt with in the mere confines of one section of a general work on drumming. I thus feel that no apology is necessary for placing yet another book upon – I hope – the library shelf of the keen drummer. I am supported in this belief by the hundreds of requests I receive for the information which is now placed on paper."[6] What Chick Webb had was an uncanny ability to listen to a run-through of his band performing a new arrangement, then immediately sitting down to his set and catch every phrase, break, and send-off,

CHICK

and perform them flawlessly. "Beverly Peer, 'He would take everything in at rehearsals, standing in front of the band or over to the side. Before long, he could tell you where every lick was supposed to happen in the new chart we were playing and just how the arrangement should sound. Once he got the thing in his mind, he never forgot *any* of it. He worked out the approach to each number at rehearsal and got further into the chart every time he played it. After a while, it seemed as if he wrote the arrangement.' Cliff Leeman, 'Chick was very specific about certain things. "When the brass is bright, you step in right up there; stay on top of the beat and play loud with the section," he said. "When the saxes are cool and laid back, you come down and play with *them*." He felt the time should be firm, but at the same time a bit flexible. "Move with the sections," he suggested. He emphasized, by example, the importance of dynamics in a big band. Moving

[6] Max Bacon, *Max On Swing* (London: The Premier Drum Co., LTD., 1934).

from very loud to very soft and vice-versa, he'd always be authoritative while supporting the band. No matter what the level of volume, Chick kept things swinging. He established a lively pulse and a variety of feelings. But he always let the music guide him. I'll never forget how effective he was when he made the change from explosive loudness to triple pianissimo. The extreme change of color was *something*.' Doc Cheatham, 'Chick was a marvelous player of breaks and figures with the trumpets. I was in the section; I know how it felt. He added impact to the ensembles, too, by backing them in core spots in an arrangement. Nobody did that until he came on the scene. Before Chick, drummers were essentially time-keepers. He was the first one to get away from the old concept and move into a more expressive way of playing.' Gene Krupa, 'I found direction when I first heard Chick. He changed everything around for me, not long after I came to New York. Why? He thought in an original way and knew exactly what to do, particularly in a big band. All of us in that 'learnin' groove' in the 1930's were enlightened by him.' Dave Tough, 'Chick Webb does everything there is to be done to a drum and does it beautifully and sometimes he played with such stupefying technique that he leaves you in a punch drunk stupor and ecstatically bewildered as this sentence has wound up to be.' Buddy Rich, 'Chick was hell on up-tempos. He kept the time firm and exciting, tapping out an even 4/4 on the bass drum. That was *something* in the 1930's. Most guys downtown could hardly make two beats to the bar; they were into the Chicago style – Dixieland. Chick set an example. He was hip, sharp, swinging.' Jo Jones, 'when everybody else would be going to after-hours spots, I would be with Mr. Webb. He would be talking, but I would be listening. He'd show me and then come...and check me out.'[7] Webb went on to record three more sessions in 1934 while maintaining a busy touring schedule planned around his contract as the house band at the Savoy. Chick fell in love with Martha Loretta "Sally" Ferguson, a hostess at the Savoy and they were married that summer. "Webb's income was now such that he was able to rent a house on 'Stivers' Row' at 120 West 138th street, ironically near to his great rival and admirer, Fletcher Henderson (also not far from the Savoy). His self-reliance had increased too, and he now had his own car (a white Cadillac) and a chauffeur-cum-manservant Joe Saunders to take care of tasks he found difficult because of his deformity. Yet despite the growing financial security, the move into the big time remained tantalizingly beyond his grasp. His career had reached a significant crossroad."[8] Yet another Savoy battle February 2, 1935 with Willie Bryant and His Orchestra, pit Webb up against drummer Cozy Cole. Cole was one of the first drummers to record a drum solo in Jelly Roll Morton's Red Hot Peppers' "Load Of Cole" in 1930. Notwithstanding, Webb was the victor in the evening. He was also victorious in his next battle April 24 against Glen Gray and the Casa Loma Orchestra with Tony Briglia on drums. In fact, Webb supposedly won all but one battle in his career. This did not seem to thwart his rivals from entering into the fray either on Webb's home turf at the Savoy in Harlem or on the road. Webb used the term "Spinnin' the Webb" to describe attracting his competition and audiences.

COZY COLE

THE CASA LOMA ORCHESTRA

[7] Burt Korall, *Drummin' Men* (New York: Schirmer Books, 1990).
[8] Stuart Nicholson, *Ella Fitzgerald* (London: Victor Gollancz, 1993).

125th STREET
APOLLO
AMERICA'S SMARTEST COLORED SHOWS!!
THEATRE 425th STREET NEAR 8th AV
TELEPHONE UN 4-4490
ONE WEEK ONLY
BEGINNING
FRIDAY, APRIL 9th
CLARENCE ROBINSON
Producer of the New
COTTON CLUB REVUE
Presents
CHICK WEBB AND HIS BAND
with the greatest of all Sepia crooners and Swing Singers
ELLA FITZGERALD
AND A FINE SUPPORTING REVUE CAST
MORTON & MARGO — COOK & BROWN — WOLFORD'S PETS
Favorites
Ensemble Dancers
Sensational Dog Act
"PIGMEAT" — JOHN MASON — JIMMIE BASKETTE
WHITE'S LINDYMANIACS — HILDA PERLENO — 16 DANCING DAMSELS
also "MIDNIGHT COURT" A STIRRING DRAMA OF CROOKS AND THE LAW
MIDNIGHT SHOW SATURDAY
ADDED ACTS Reserved Seats now on Sale
WED. — AMATEURNIGHT
BROADCAST FROM STAGE
ONE WEEK — BEGINNING FRIDAY, APRIL 16th
DON REDMAN
AND HIS ORCHESTRA
with LOUISE McCARROL
3 BERRY BROS.
CHUCK & CHUCKLES

BACK AT THE
SAVOY BALLROOM
NEXT SAT. NITE
The Home Of Happy Feet • Lenox Ave. At 140th St.
gale, INC. R.K.O. BLDG. RADIO CITY, NEW YORK CITY
presents
Chick WEBB
and his Orchestra
featuring
ELLA FITZGERALD
Tour Direction: CONSOLIDATED RADIO ARTISTS, Inc. NEW YORK – CLEVELAND – CHICAGO – DALLAS – HOLLYWOOD

ELLA

When Webb proposed adding Ella to the orchestra, Moe Gale balked. Seeing "a shy and awkward teenager. He said 'No!' 'Listen to the voice,' Webb told him. 'Don't look at her.' Gale listened and she was hired."

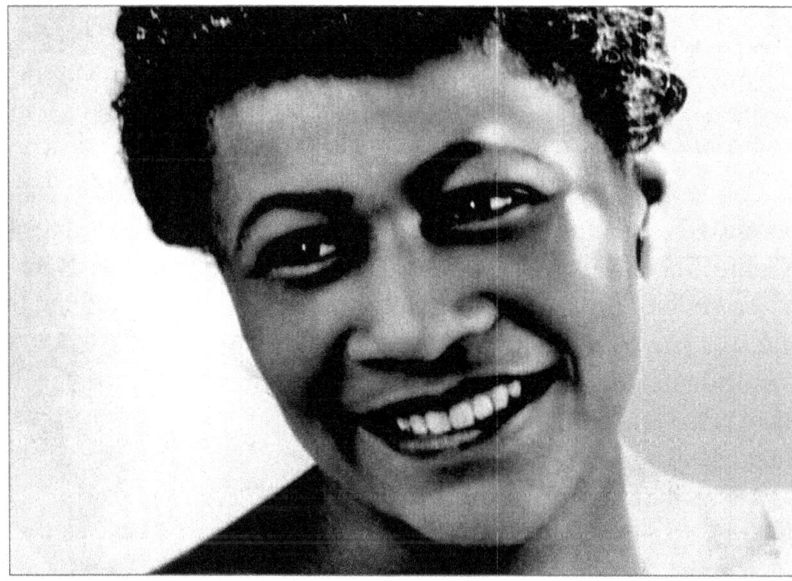

ELLA FITZGERALD

Stuart Nicholson began his acclaimed 1993 biography of Ella Fitzgerald with, "Ella Fitzgerald has lived to sing. Nothing in her life has meant so much to her. It has been the focus of her whole being, sustaining her career at the top of her profession for seven decades. Her vocal style, widely acknowledged as a touchstone of excellence, has been admired for its purity of tone, clarity of diction, harmonic imagination and a highly refined sense of swing."[1] Ella Jane Fitzgerald was born out of wedlock, April 25, 1917 in Newport News, Virginia. Soon after, her father William abandoned Ella and her mother Tempie. Tempie found another man, Joe Da Silva, an immigrant from Portugal and in search of a better life, the family moved to Yonkers, New York. Within a few years, Tempie and Joe had another daughter, Francine Da Silva, with whom Ella would remain close for life. Typical of the underprivileged then and now, Ella's day-to-day existence was meager at best. Though a good student, Ella did not participate in any school music programs. Still, like all teenagers, music was a big part of her life. Her favorite popular artists were Louis Armstrong and the Boswell Sisters, particularly Connee Boswell. "'She was tops at the time,' said Ella in 1988, 'I was attracted to her immediately. My mother brought home one of her records and I fell in love with it. I tried so hard to sound just like her.' 'When I was a girl I listened to records by all the singers, white and black. And I know that Connee Boswell was doing things that no one else was doing at the time. You don't have to take my word for it. Just check the recordings and hear for yourself.'"[2] One of the things Fitzgerald was so impressed with was Armstrong and Boswell's ability to "scat." "Scat singing is a difficult technique that requires singers with the ability to sing improvised melodies and rhythms using the voice as an instrument rather than a speaking medium."[3] Though there are earlier examples of scat, the grandfather is Louis Armstrong with his recording of "Heebie Jeebies" in 1926. It is reported that while recording the tune, Armstrong's music fell on the floor. Rather than stopping the session, he continued on, improvising the melody using his voice as an instrument. Many people have tried scatting, but few have succeeded to the level of Armstrong, Boswell and later, Fitzgerald. In 1932 Ella's mother died abruptly and Ella moved in with her Aunt Virginia in Harlem. In both Yonkers and Harlem, young Ella would often impress her peers with her interpretation of Armstrong

[1] Ibid.
[2] Ibid.
[3] No author credited. "Scat singing," http://en.wikipedia.org/wiki/Scat_singing

APOLLO, HARLEM, NEW YORK (WONDER IF BIG SID NOTICED)

and Boswell's styles. Fitzgerald's ambitions though were in dance and finding some success at the Lafayette Theatre talent contest, she went on to try her hand at the Apollo Theatre located at 125th Street and Seventh Avenue. Rather than prize money being awarded at Amateur Night at the Apollo, winners were given the unique honor of a week's engagement at the theatre.

Full of ambition, Ella entered the competition Wednesday, November 24, 1934 in the dance category. When she arrived at the Monday night audition, she wisely anticipated her chances of winning were nil against a semi-professional dance team. Quickly changing her category to singer, she nervously took the stage. After a false start she was permitted to begin again and sufficiently impressed the judges to win the audition and go on to the Amateur Night. Ella chose "The Object Of My Affection" and "Judy" for her stage debut. Fitzgerald's performance, in the style of Connee Boswell, was enthusiastically received by the audience that night and to her surprise, she was the overwhelming winner. Unfortunately the theatre reneged on the weeks' engagement, supposedly due to her ragged appearance. Ella's adoptive home proved unsettling and she spent most of her time on the streets of Harlem. As a result she took on a homeless appearance, performing at the Apollo in a second-hand dress and men's boots. An audition arranged with Fletcher Henderson proved disastrous for the same reason. Although Ella was booed off the stage at the Lafayette Theatre Amateur Night, she tenaciously forged on with an appearance at yet another Amateur Night at the Harlem Opera House. Her performance of "Judy" again won the approval of the audience and she was victorious for the evening. Though the promised week's engagement at the Opera House was fulfilled, Fitzgerald received no pay as the management deducted the cost of a "suitable" stage dress.

ELLA

History is a little vague as to who brought Fitzgerald to Webb's attention, either Charles Linton, Webb's current singer - which seems unlikely, the Great Depression was still in full swing, hardly an environment for such a gratuitous gesture - or Webb's bandleader, Bardu Ali. Regardless, Webb was under pressure from Savoy's Charles Buchanan and Moe Gale, now Chick Webb's manager, to recruit a female singer to broaden the appeal of the Chick Webb Orchestra. Every effort to this point, new arrangements, changing personnel, did not generate the mass appeal enjoyed by the likes of Duke Ellington, Louis Armstrong, or Benny Goodman. Though a sensation at his home turf on the Savoy, Chick's kismet needed a helping hand.

BARDU ALI, ELLA FITZGERALD

Stuart Nicholson, "a young girl who had asked for his autograph just a few months earlier, was going to play a remarkable role in moving his (Webb's) career out of the doldrums and establishing the Chick Webb Orchestra as one of the nation's top big bands. That young girl was Ella Fitzgerald."[4] When Webb proposed adding Ella to the orchestra, Moe Gale balked. Seeing "a shy and awkward teenager. He said 'No!' 'Listen to the voice,' Webb told him. 'Don't look at her.' Gale listened and she was hired."[5] Webb is quoted, "Now I hope she is willing to be taught a few things." Some accounts attempt to discredit Webb's discovery of Fitzgerald, claiming her voice would have inevitably garnered the fame she richly deserved. Though this is probably true, it was her association with the Webb organization, including the management of Moe Gale, the accompanying top musicians, Van Alexander's timely arrangements, and above all, Webb's judicious musical instincts that jump-started her seven-decade career. Eighteen-year-old Ella was officially onboard with the Webb Orchestra, May of 1935. With the help of Chick's management and band members, Ella was transformed into a stage personality. Dress, hair, make up, whatever it took to make her "presentable" was provided…but it was her voice that succeeded above all else. Webb sensed he had a "diamond in the rough" and included her in his next recording session a few weeks later. An instrumental arrangement by Wayne Carver "Down Home Rag," was followed by two vocals arranged by Edgar Sampson. The first, aptly named "Are You Here To Stay?" sung by Charles Linton, then Ella's "Love And Kisses," was the beginning of her fruitful recording career. On July 28, 1935 Ella participated in her first Battle of the Bands when Chick and the orchestra dueled with Julie Wintz Palisades Band with George Zimmer on drums at Palisades Amusement Park, Fort Lee, NJ. An October 1935 Decca session yielded three more Ella vocals, a Taft Jordan (one of Chick's trumpeters) vocal, and an instrumental. Two days later, Webb took on Buddy Johnson's Band in a mêlée in his hometown of Baltimore, then on October 27 he traveled to the Cotton Club in Nashville, Tennessee to do battle with the Ruth Ellington Orchestra. Later, Webb added Charles Linton to two recording session vocal lineups, but aside from an occasional use of one of the band members for vocals, for the remainder of Chick's sessions, Ella Fitzgerald was the staple. In fact, of the 21 subsequent recording sessions, Webb recorded 82 cuts using Ella

CHICK'S CHICK

It's the latest pose of Ella Fitzgerald, popular warbler with Chick Webb's band. What a grin!

ELLA, METRONOME MAGAZINE

[4] Stuart Nicholson, *Ella Fitzgerald* (London: Victor Gollancz, 1993).

[5] John McDonough, "The Complete Chick Webb & Ella Fitzgerald Decca Sessions (1934-1941)," Mosaic Records, July 2013.

exclusively, while only recording 14 instrumentals. Priorities were set. Including Moe Gale convincing NBC Radio to air his live production of "Good Time Society" Saturday nights, sometimes from Radio City Music Hall in downtown Manhattan. Radio airplay insured chart-making exposure for artists and Chick was quick to take notice, convincing NBC Radio to add another seven weekly appearances. Thousands of fan letters arrived every week making Chick and Ella instant celebrities.

THIS PHOTO OF ELLA AND CHICK WAS TAKEN THE NIGHT OF THE GOODMAN/ WEBB BATTLE

Continuing in the "Battle Mad" mode, Webb's next clash November 3, 1935 was on a road trip against the Jimmy Noone Orchestra at the Savoy Ballroom in Chicago with Johnny Wells on drums. Noone's Orchestra, a local favorite, offered little competition. It was during these grueling road trips over the next few months that Ella became solid with the Webb songbook. Like her mentor Webb, Ella had the uncanny ability to listen to an arrangement once, then immediately render an exact performance with ease. Returning as the house band at the Savoy, the Webb Orchestra with singer Ella Fitzgerald, resumed recording at Decca in April of 1936. Back on the road again, Webb scheduled another battle June 12 against his old friend Fletcher Henderson with Kaiser Marshall on drums at the 8th Regiment Armory, Chicago, IL. Erskine Tate Orchestra with Jimmie Bertrand/drums and Don Redman Orchestra with Manzie Johnson/drums were also on the bill. During June and October recording sessions, two hits were birthed and Chick Webb finally saw his name on the charts. "Sing Me A Swing Song (And Let Me Dance)" reached number 18 and later, "(If You Can't Sing It) You'll Have To Swing It," in which Ella scats for the first time, rose to number 20. Ella was gaining recognition in her own right and not only as Chick Webb's vocalist. In fact, the following recording session in November was labeled as "Ella Fitzgerald And Her Savoy Eight." This rising stardom attracted the attention of not only her adoring fans but also Webb's rivals. Benny Goodman had just recorded his version of "Sing Me A Swing Song" a few months earlier and took notice of Ella. His vocalist, Helen Ward was on leave when Goodman asked Ella to record three cuts with him in November, "Good Night My Love," "Take Another Guess," and "Did You Mean It?" at Victor Records. When "Did You Mean It?" was released a few weeks later all hell broke lose. Decca summoned their attorneys and a legal battle followed, resulting in Victor withdrawing the release from their catalogue. Ella went on to do several live radio broadcasts with Goodman. Seeing her potential, Goodman offered $5,000 in an attempt to add Ella to his team. In the January 14, 1937 *Pittsburgh Courier* article "The Truth About Ella's $5,000 Offer," correspondent Edgar Rouzean reports that while performing at the Pennsylvania Hotel in New York, Webb said "He (Goodman) has been trying to get Ella in the worst way. I turned him down."[6] Ella also entertained a lucrative offer from Jimmie Lunceford until both were immediately halted when Moe Gale stepped in with his contract signed by Fitzgerald. Everyone was clamoring to join the Ella bandwagon.

It is likely that Chick changed his drum set about the time Ella joined the band. Though no photographs exist of Chick's prior complete Leedy set (only the snare drum), after Ella joined the band, photos of Chick

[6] Edgar Rouzean, "The Truth About Ella's $5,000 Offer" (*Pittsburgh Courier*, January 14, 1937).

are with a Frank Wolf drum set in a sparkle (probably green) finish. The drums consisted of a large (huge by today's standards) 14 by 28 inch bass drum, a 12 by 14 inch tom mounted on his right side and a 6 ½ by 14 inch snare drum. The Wolf snare drum was unique in its day. Called a "2 to 1 Tension Snare Drum" it featured 12 tension rods and lugs on top head and 6 on the bottom head. Normally, drums have equal tension rods on both the top and bottom heads. This design principal Wolf developed supposedly accommodated the higher tension required for the top of the snare drum with more tension apparatus. All drums were mounted on a Premier Drum Company (from England) rolling console that included gooseneck cymbal arms. Though the wheels on the console had locking breaks, Webb's forceful playing required additional locking spurs attached to the bass drum to keep it in place. Chick's cymbal set up consisted of a 15 inch China with rivets on his far right, a 13 inch Avedis Zildjian above, a 12 inch Avedis Zildjian on his left and a pair of 12 inch Avedis Zildjian Hi Hat Cymbals. The Zildjian Company has been in continuous operation since 1623, first in Turkey, then also in the USA. In 1929 the "secret formula" was passed down to the oldest living male heir, Avedis Zildjian, an American immigrant. Avedis set about changing the formula somewhat when leading jazz drummers advised the cymbals needed to be thinner/ lighter. Heretofore, cymbals were thicker and heavier for band and orchestral applications. As a result, cymbals became "paper-thin." "In the 1930's, with the Zildjian trademark becoming as prominent a brand in percussion as Ludwig or Slingerland, the top name drummers made the trip to Norfolk Downs (Quincy, Massachusetts) to meet with Avedis (founder) and chose from a special selection of the magical bronze discs. Armand (Avedis' son) remembers Cliff Leeman, Jimmy Crawford, and the supremely gifted and influential Chick Webb all coming through the doors of his father's factory. 'Chick almost stood while he was playing he was so short,' says Armand Zildjian. 'There weren't many jazz drummers that suspended their cymbals, just Chick (Mr. Zildjian is mistaken here, the suspension system was used by several others). He was a very mild guy to talk to. He loved cymbals and loved the drums.'"[7] Mounted on the "trap" table in the center of Chick's console were four Chinese temple blocks, a cowbell, and a wood block. "Cliff Leeman, 'Chick worked on his drums all the time. Like most of the great players of the time, he tuned his drums in a highly

"Who Dat Man?" Dat man be Little Chickie Webbie just coming out of a super-mergentroid rim-shot.

CHICK, METRONOME MAGAZINE

[7] Jon Cohan, *Zildjian, A History of the Legendary Cymbal Makers* (Milwaukee: Hal Leonard, 1999).

intelligent manner, so as to get different sonorities from various parts of the set. His bass drum work set an example for all other drummers. He played the big drum *open*. By that I mean he didn't resort to padding to muffle it and make it easier to control. To further enhance its full, warm sound, he used tympani heads on both sides of the drum. He allowed the drum to naturally resonate. He had great control of his right foot, which was very strong and flexible. Chick could perform miracles with his foot, achieving great speed and various levels of sound. Roy Eldridge, 'Chick and most of the really good drummers in the 1930s used to tune their bass drum to a G on the bass fiddle. They *controlled* the bass drum and what they played blended with the bass. Hey, did you know that Chick was the first guy I ever heard who dropped bombs, the way the boppers did later on.'"[8] Another interesting thing about Chick's bass drum was the painting on the front head. Before drum sets were even conceived, the large expanse of the bass drum head cried out for decoration. Civil War drummers painted their regimental identification. Later, New Orleans Jazz drummers branded their band's name, followed by bass drum heads decorated with all sorts of colorful images, landscapes, windmills, boats, dancing ladies, every imaginable embellishment to enhance the band's image. Gene Krupa, with the Benny Goodman Orchestra, was one of the first to stencil his initials in a shield and stripe ornamentation on the left of the bass drum head with large BG initials on the right, a decoration adopted by many drummers for years to come. Chick's image was unique. Though other drummers emblazoned their bass drum head with a facial image of the group's leader, Chick opted for a more cartoon caricature likeness, specifically one supplied by Barend "Boy" ten Hove. Ten Hove began his creative art career in a small town in the Netherlands aptly named Haarlem. "Being a jazz (record) collector Boy moved to Haarlem at the right time. In the thirties it already had an important jazz scene."[9] Ten Hove's early work appeared in *De Jazzwereld* and *Rhythm* magazines. Commodore Record's Milt Gabler discovered Ten Hove's work and hung images of Duke Ellington, Fats Waller, Louis Armstrong, Count Basie and others throughout his record shop on 42nd Street in New York. It was probably there, or Chick saw the same image in a 1936 issue of *Rhythm* magazine and decided to have it painted on the front of his bass drum. "This drawing (minus the crown, more about that later) was also used to promote dances at the Savoy Ballroom."[10]

Boy ten Hove's caricatures by Ate van Delden

Milt Gabler's Commodore Music Shop on Forty Second Street

[8] Burt Korall, *Drummin' Men* (New York: Schirmer Books, 1990).

[9] Ate van Delden, *Boy ten Hove's caricatures* (Zaltbommel, Holland: Uitgeverij Aprilis Books, 2006).

[10] Ibid.

THE MUSICAL BATTLE OF THE CENTURY

"Billy Taylor, 'Chick and Sid Catlett and Jo Jones had something important in common. They were all great showmen. These guys came up when the drummer and everybody, for that matter, had to hold his own spot. If you had a spot in a show in a theatre or club and you didn't get as much applause as the juggler, singer, or shake dancer, then you lost that feature. That's why drummers threw sticks and did all kinds of show biz things, while they tried to play in a marvelous musical manner. Chick was in the forefront because he knew exactly how to deal with that situation.' Dicky Wells, 'I remember playing a week with Chick once when Big Green (Charlie Green) was ill. It was at the Lafayette Theatre in Harlem. Well, I was down front and the people were applauding and I was bowing and thinking it pretty nice, when something struck me to turn around, and there was Chick really breaking the joint up. He could break up a show any time he wanted. He'd start hunching his shoulders, and throwing sticks, and really playing.'"[1] Davey Tough, then drummer with Tommy Dorsey, was not a stick twirler. In fact, if you saw Tough on the bandstand you'd probably wonder how a banker got the gig; he was that sedate. Burt Korall, "Tough made no compromises. An unconventional player almost entirely lacking in technique, he had no interest in showmanship. Musicality, pulsation, and the beauty of a highly integrated ensemble performance were his concerns. Fans found it easier to cement a link with drummers like Webb, Krupa, Rich, (Jo) Jones, and Sidney Catlett, whose showmanship and technical gifts were very appealing. Things haven't changed too radically since then."[2] No wonder then, the Webb/Dorsey Battle at the Savoy on December 13, 1936 was a foregone conclusion. Webb, a superb player with a knack for the drama won the evening. But you can bet he kept a watchful eye on Tough's marvelous playing that night. The audience may not have appreciated Tough's talents but as Woody Herman notes, "A great rhythm player! With the least amount of 'chops,' Dave inspired a whole, big screamin' band with his subtleties and strong feeling for time. And he was probably one of the most gentle, the kindest, one of the grooviest cats you'd ever want to know."[3] While Chick was mindful of his competition, he was also holding back. Seeing this, "Dorsey's men said, 'Come on, Chick. Show us some stuff.' And Chick smiled and responded, 'No, I'm waiting.' As Dorsey's publicist, the late Jack

DAVE TOUGH

[1] Burt Korall, *Drummin' Men* (New York: Schirmer Books, 1990).

[2] Ibid.

[3] Ibid.

Egan, told me, 'Chick was playing possum.'"[4] Chick was saving his reserves for his upcoming battles with Fletcher Henderson, Duke Ellington, and especially the "King of Swing," the mega star, Benny Goodman. Based on Webb's comment, Goodman had already accepted the invitation to do battle in Harlem. Popular sentiment was with Goodman as he had the number one band in the country. *Metronome* published an ongoing "Dance Band Review" by George Simon. The review consisted of an "A" to "C-" rating system. In the January, 1938 *Metronome* article "Only Six Bands Have Copped Straight "A" Ratings," Simon writes, "Besides Duke Ellington, Benny Goodman, Bob Crosby, Red Norvo (small band), Ray Noble, and Al Kavelin are the only bands who have received 'A' awards during the history of Dance Band Reviews. A complete table of bands, the issue in which each was reviewed, and rating received follows: (under the rating of "A"), "Bob Crosby (April, '36); Duke Ellington (June, '37); Benny Goodman (June, '35); Al Kavelin (Nov., '35); Ray Noble (July, '35); Red Norvo (March, '36)."[5] Goodman was the first to receive an "A" rating in 1935 with Webb receiving a B+ in that same June issue. One can only imagine Chick's anticipation of the scheduled upcoming May 11, 1937 battle with Goodman. Chick's busy recording schedule continued with a Decca session just before the Dorsey battle and one just prior to the February 28, 1937 battle against Fletcher Henderson. Against Henderson's new drummer, Walter Johnson, Webb probably didn't even work up a sweat. On March 3rd Chick had a pick-up session at Variety Records recording two cuts with Jimmy Mundy and his Swing Club Seven. Four days later he found himself facing his old pal Duke in a touch-and-go battle at the Savoy. Reflecting on the night, "Teddy McRae, 'I think five windows broke at the Savoy that night. So much weight going up and down, you know. Everybody jumping on the same beat. It was really a terrific battle. Chick said 'We're gonna work hard. The place is full.' Someone said, 'You all ain't gonna make no more money. Just play.' Chick wouldn't hear of it: 'No one gonna come here and lay down. Everyone has to work. You're up here in my nest.' Sandy Williams, 'We had the reputation of running out any band which came into the Savoy. But not Duke's. When we opened we broke up the house. Then he started, and he'd go from one tune right into another. The whole room was swinging right along with him. I looked and saw Chick sneaking into the office. 'I can't take it,' he said. 'This is the first time we've ever really been washed out.' You're right Boss Man, I said. They're laying it on us tonight! In fact, they outswung and out-everythinged us.'"[6] Two things probably contributed to Chick's defeat that night. First, the Ellington Orchestra's

BENNY GOODMAN "THE KING OF SWING"

SAVOY DANCERS

[4] Ibid.
[5] George Simon, "Only Six Bands Have Copped Straight "A" Ratings," *Metronome*, January 1938.
[6] Burt Korall, *Drummin' Men* (New York: Schirmer Books, 1990).

busy tour schedule (including Europe) and Cotton Club performances honed the ensemble's swing skills. Ellington was about to be named the number one band in the country. Second was Webb's undoubted preoccupation with defeating Benny Goodman in two months. Goodman, after all, tried to steal away Ella, Chick's perceived ticket to success. Webb's next recording session at Decca yielded six Ella vocals and two instrumentals, one of which the swinging Edgar Sampson arrangement of "Clap Hands, Here Comes Charlie." Webb sustains this up-tempo cut with a swinging hi hat, then switches to rim clicks during the piano solo. He ends with a driving 2 and 4 on the China cymbal followed by a quick change-up to a half-time final measure. The next day's session at Variety Records was the Gotham Stompers, a group that consisted of members of Chick and Ellington's Orchestras.

Gene Krupa "Ace Drummer Man"

Chick was also preoccupied with Goodman's drummer, Gene Krupa. They shared many similar experiences. Born in the same year as Webb, Krupa decided to play drums at age 11 while working at Brown's Music Company in Chicago. He later shared the drum seat with Dave Tough in the so-called Austin High Gang, a local group of young, aspiring musicians. Krupa and Tough sampled the local Jazz spots in Chicago's South Side, including the "Three Deuces" where Krupa met Benny Goodman. Drummers they saw were Zutty Singleton, Tubby Hall, and Baby Dodds who Krupa most favored and emulated in his playing. His first recording at Okeh Records was in 1927 with members of the Austin High Gang. Along with his pal guitarist Eddie Condon, Gene made the move to the Big Apple in 1928 where he recorded with Red Nichols and Miff Mole while playing in various dance orchestras. In 1934 record producer John Hammond recruited Krupa to join the newly formed Benny Goodman Orchestra that featured arrangements by Fletcher Henderson. The Goodman/Krupa recording of *Sing Sing Sing* in 1936 was an instant hit and became another anthem in the annals of Swing. Krupa's movie-star good looks paired with his thrilling on-stage performance, attracted women by the droves. Later, he had his own column in *Metronome* magazine. When Goodman accepted Chick's challenge to do battle on the fields of Harlem, he and Krupa were number one. Benny demanded the large main bandstand at the Savoy for the showdown. Chick accepted. Benny demanded rehearsal time at the Savoy prior to the battle. Chick accepted. With all the elements in place, it was time for promotion. "Helen Oakley Dance, 'I was doing publicity for Chick and wanted to do something that was really newsworthy. I laid one on. Of course it was a forgone conclusion in a way because no matter what

Spinning the web! Moe Gale, manager of Chick Webb's Chicks, talking stuff with his new associate, Helen Oakley, former Benny Goodman war-time correspondent from the Chicago front.

Helen Oakley Dance and Moe Gale, Metronome Magazine

THE MUSICAL SENSATION OF 1937, BENNY GOODMAN/CHICK WEBB BATTLE OF THE BANDS

Benny had up his sleeve, and no matter how hard Gene worked, they really didn't have a chance against Chick in his home territory.' Mario Bauza, 'When we came to work that night, Chick said, "Fellows, I don't have to tell you this is the biggest thing that's going to happen to us. Tonight we got to make history. Our future depends on tonight. So I don't want any excuses. I don't want nobody drunk. I don't want nobody to miss; anybody do any little thing wrong, don't look for me to give you notice. Just pack and go home because this is my life."' The headline in *Down Beat* was "Call Out Riot Squad to Handle Mob at Goodman-Webb Battle." All-time Savoy records were broken. More than 4,000 got into the ballroom and 5,000 were turned away. Because the crowds were so large and enthusiastic, the Savoy management had to call the riot squad, the fire department, reserves, and mounted police to keep the people in check. In the area surrounding, traffic was held up for hours."[7] *Metronome*'s George Simon noted a highlight of the evening was "Ella Fitzgerald's singing, with the crowd locking arms and swaying to and fro before her."[8] "Roy Eldridge, 'Everybody was waiting to see what happened between Chick and Gene. Gene worked hard and played good; he even broke one of his drum heads. But he couldn't do anything with Chick. The little man was mean, baby. He was mean!' Taft Jordan, 'You never heard such playing. Chick and Gene Krupa really went at it. Before the night was over, Gene stood up on Benny's stand and bowed to Chick, as if to say, "You're the King." No one on earth could have taken it away from Chick that night. This band battle was one of my greatest musical thrills.' The crowds outside the Savoy did not disperse until well after midnight. 'The climax and thrill of the evening,' says Helen Oakley Dance, 'was provided by Chick Webb who, in answer to requests, followed Benny with Benny's own hit number, "Jam Session," and blew the roof off the house with it.'"[9] The headline in the June issue of *Metronome* was "Chick Webb Defeats Benny Goodman!" Gene Krupa was later quoted. "I'll never forget that night – he just cut me to ribbons – made me feel awfully small. That man was dynamic; he could reach the most amazing heights. When he really let go, you had the feeling that the entire atmosphere in the place was charged. When he felt like it, he could cut down any of us."[10]

THIS PHOTO OF GENE KRUPA WAS ALLEGEDLY TAKEN THE NIGHT OF THE GOODMAN/WEBB BATTLE

[7] Burt Korall, *Drummin' Men* (New York: Schirmer Books, 1990).
[8] George Simon, *Metronome*, June 1937).
[9] Burt Korall, *Drummin' Men* (New York: Schirmer Books, 1990).
[10] No author credited, *Swinging At Decca – Chick Webb and his Orchestra*, http://www.virtualvictrola.com/chick-webb/

A NEW KING

CHICK WEBB

GENE KRUPA

Was Webb's exhilarating battle with Goodman an overwhelming victory? Most definitely. Can the same be said about his skirmish with Krupa? Probably not. Both Chick and Gene had very similar drumming styles, visually electrifying, sonically explosive. Krupa was "The Ace Drummer Man"; Webb was the "King of the Savoy." "Henry Adler, 'Gene was the epitome of what you would expect in a drummer. The guy was beautiful-looking…And when he played solos in his own particular, easily identifiable style, people would come out of the woodwork.'"[1] The night was an exchange of bombastic volleys, each drummer/warrior trying to outdo one another, driving those who were present, especially drummers, into a frenzy. In typical fashion the press rewrote history and appointed Chick the "King of the Drums." The name stuck. Webb returned to the Decca Studios late that May to record five fruitful sessions yielding fourteen vocals with Ella and eight instrumentals including a Charlie Dixon arrangement of "Harlem Congo." This is the first recording that we get a glimpse of what Webb was capable of, an up-tempo piece where Chick executes snare send-offs and heavy fours on bass drum. He then plays a 24 bar solo ending with a quick change up to a half time tempo for one measure, kicking-off an 8 bar shout chorus. "Dick Vance, 'Chick had us make special arrangements for the band battles. Each one would be tailored for a certain band and a particular time in the evening. "I want one of those bullets!" That's what he would say."[2] "Harlem Congo" was Chick's ammunition for his next battles. First was a lackluster conflict while on the road again in Dayton, OH against the Noble Sissle Orchestra with Jack Carter on drums in June, then back to his home turf in Harlem to go toe to toe with Jimmy Dorsey's Orchestra in November with Ray McKinley on drums. Of concern to many was Chick's apparent surrendering of the limelight to Ella. Even his band members raised an eyebrow to his new addition. Burt Korall, "some people close to Webb felt a singer was inappropriate for Webb's band, particularly at a time when instrumental jazz was beginning to enjoy such success with the advent of Benny Goodman and his band. Helen Oakley Dance, 'Chick had been totally immersed in the *band*. And the guys stood behind him 100%. But after he got Ella, it was different, because his point-of-view had changed. He began to see there could be a commercial future for the band. No doubt he adored the way she sang. Pre Ella, there was no one on that level. Chick knew exactly what he had. But I regretted the change because it meant that the band and Chick had to take a back seat. I hated for that to happen. She really *dominated.* The band played a smaller roll and its character was changing. I used to argue about it with Chick all the time. But he was committed to go his own way. I thought if I did something to bring the situation to the public's attention, it would sting him. You know, he hated to be downed in any way. And I thought if I could get to him, things might get a little better. So I arranged the battle of music between Basie and Chick. The presumption was

CHICK WEBB VS. COUNT BASIE

[1] Burt Korall, *Drummin' Men* (New York: Schirmer Books, 1990).

[2] Ibid.

CHICK WEBB "KING OF THE DRUMS," ELLA FITZGERALD "FIRST LADY OF SWING"

that we had faith that Chick would hold his own the way he always did at the Savoy. But I knew perfectly well that he wouldn't because, after all, Basie had the greatest swing band around and nothing would stop him from swinging *anybody* out of the place. That's just what happened. Webb was mad as anything and the whole band felt the same way. I believe I got fired. Or Chick threatened to fire me. I've forgotten. Everyone thought what I had done was unforgivable. But I thought of it as just a way of making my point."[3] January 16, 1938 "The King Of The Drums" crossed swords with "The Royalist Of The Keyboard" Count Basie with "Papa" Jo Jones on drums. "Milt Hinton, 'I never felt better playing than when Jo was in the rhythm section.'" (But it was)"'The All American Rhythm Section' of Basie, (guitarist Walter) Page, (bassist Freddie) Green, and Jones (that) had its own recipe. Relaxing, being natural, responding consonantly and with feeling to the music – all of this gave the section distinction. The beautiful part, though, was that each person in the section never forgot who and what he was, or what a variegated role his instrument could play."[4] The evening was an eventful one for several reasons. While Webb and Basie were doing battle uptown at the Savoy, Benny Goodman was headlining at the first jazz concert in history downtown at Carnegie Hall. Supposedly after the Goodman concert there was a caravan of noted jazz royalty making its way uptown for the battle, including Basie, Ellington, Goodman with most of his band in tow (including Krupa), Mildred Bailey, Red Norvo, and others. But the evening's events were not just about the battle between Chick and the Count, or Goodman's Carnegie Hall concert, it was also about two ladies, "Lady Day" and the "First Lady Of Swing." Notice in the illustration the monikers "The King Of The Drums" for Chick and "The First Lady Of Swing" for Ella (courtesy of Dave Brown). Billie Holiday aka "Lady Day" was two years older than Ella and similarly, got her start as a singer in Harlem. When Ella was auditioning for the Amateur Night at the Apollo, Billie had already established herself singing in various

"PAPA" JO JONES

WEBB "CUTS" BASIE IN SWING BATTLE

New York, N. Y.—The much heralded Battle of Swing between Chick Webb's and Count Basie's bands took place Sunday night, Jan. 16, at the Savoy Ballroom. The affair drew a record attendance and hundreds were turned away at the box office, with the crowds tying up traffic for several blocks in that vicinity. Applause for both bands was tremendous and it was difficult to determine which band was the more popular.

Nevertheless, the ballot taken showed Chick Webb's band well in the lead over Basie's and Ella Fitzgerald well out in front over Billie Holliday and James Rushing. The battle took place after Benny Goodman's concert at Carnegie Hall, and many of Benny Goodman's band, including Gene Krupa, Lionel Hampton, Jimmie Mundy, Hymie Scherzer and others were present. Mildred Bailev, Red Norvo, Teddy Hill, Willie Bryant, Eddie Duchin, Duke Ellington and Ivie Anderson were also on hand.

Basie Sends Dancers While Webb Steals Show on Drums

DOWN BEAT MAGAZINE, FEBRUARY 1938

LOUIS ARMSTRONG AND BILLIE HOLIDAY

[3] Ibid.
[4] Ibid.

Basie's Brilliant Band Conquers Chick's

Newspaper Men Give Decision to Count Over Webb in Savoy Battle . . . Solid Swings to Heart Triumph Over Sensational Blows to Head

Count Basie did it! For years nobody was able to lick Chick Webb and his Chicks within the walls of his home Savoy Ballroom, but on January 16, right after Benny Goodman's concert further downtown in Carnegie Hall, a milling throng, that included such notables as Duke Ellington, Red Norvo, Mildred Bailey, Eddy Duchin, Gene Krupa, Lionel Hampton and the Benny Goodman family jammed into Harlem's Hottest Hot House to see and hear the Count gain a newspapermen's decision over the famed Chick.

Basie had everything that night! Seldom has any band, any place, cut loose with such unmitigated swing the way the Count's Cohorts did that memorable eve. METRONOME, usually proud of its predictions, completed a complete turn-about-face that eve, and right now goes publicly into print with apologies to backers of the band who have been singing its potential praises for many months now, but with whom METRONOME,

(Turn to page 20, please)

Happy Birthday

We are advised that Happy Birthday of which we published on orchestra arrangement in our January issue is protected by U. S. Copyright and said Copyright is held by Clayton F. Summy Company of Chicago, Illinois. We wish to express our sincere regret that this number was inadvertently used.

METRONOME MAGAZINE, FEBRUARY 1938, PAGE 15

Harlem night spots, recording two cuts with Benny Goodman in 1933, and appearing in a Duke Ellington film short *Symphony In Black: A Rhapsody Of Negro Life*. Though Ella was just voted Number One Female Vocalist in the *Melody Maker* reader's poll, her popularity was the result of pop and novelty songs. Billie's success was in the arena of jazz with record producer John Hammond associating her style with that of Louis Armstrong, Ella's early influence. It is no wonder Ella's anticipation of the evening was one of intimidation. Still, with her motivation to be on top, like that of her partner Chick, her performance of "Loch Lomond" won over the crowd and she was crowned the winner. In fact, several accounts differ radically from Helen Oakley Dance's assessment of the battle. February 1938 issue of *Down Beat* notes "Applause for both bands was tremendous and it was difficult to determine which band was the more popular, Nevertheless, the ballot taken showed Chick Webb's band well in the lead over Basie's and Ella Fitzgerald well out in front over Billie Holiday. When Ella sang she had the whole crowd rocking with her."[5] *Metronome* seemed a bit confused on the outcome. On page 15 of the February 1938 issue the headline reads, "Basie's Brilliant Band Conquers Chick's." But then reverses itself on page 20 with another headline, "Votes Contradict Swing Critics." The article continues, "Newspaper men, notably swing critics, can be wrong so far as the public is concerned. That's what post mortems anent the Chick Webb – Count Basie Battle of Savoy brought out. The scribes, voting almost to a man for the Count, countered stiff opposition from ballotteers in the Savoy who by more than a two to one margin presented the palm to their own Chick."[6] The press was not always kind to Webb and his orchestra. *Metronome's* George Simon attended a performance at the Savoy and reported in the January 1938 issue, "as the evening wore on, it became apparent that one of the band's greatest qualities was sorely lacking. That was the general free spirit of attack, the will to give whole heartedly, a quality that has always been one of the strong selling-points of the Webbian presentation. Somehow or other you began to feel as if the band were beginning to hi-hat hot Harlem: that its successful appearances in all parts of the land had become to have their psychological effect, and now that the band was becoming a national institution, it was beginning to consider itself too good for its Savoy Stalwarts – who had given it its original start. It was playing down to the Savoy dancers, and if any band should play up to them, that band should be Chick's. Here's uttering a humble prayer that this truly great Chick Webb band, which can cut just about any swing outfit in the world, won't turn into one of those stiff, stagey aggregations, which measures glory in terms of quarts of grease paint and number of orchestra seats sold per performance."[7]

THE METRONOME

Count Basie

Votes Contradict Swing Critics

Webb Really Cut Basie, Small Savoy Balloting Avers, Placing Blasts Above Grooves

Newspaper men, notably swing critics, can be wrong so far as the general public is concerned. That's what post mortems anent the Chick Webb-Count Basie Battle of Savoy brought out. The scribes, voting almost to a man for the Count, countered stiff opposition from ballotteers in the Savoy who by more than a two to one margin presented the palm to their own Chick.

METRONOME MAGAZINE, FEBRUARY 1938, PAGE 20

[5] No author credited, "Webb 'Cuts' Basie In Swing Battle," *Down Beat*, February 1938.

[6] No author credited, "Basie's Brilliant Band Conquers Chick's" and "Votes Contradict Swing Critics," *Metronome*, February 1938.

[7] George Simon, "Roasts And Toasts," *Metronome*, January 1938.

The press was also concerned that Ella was becoming too central a figure for the band, especially with her pop songs contrasting sharply with the hard-edged instrumentals the band had become known for. All this was lost on her adoring fans and her boss Chick. Webb had a grand plan for Ella and himself and did not seem concerned about the opinions of others. Ella shared that dream. It wasn't all about business though. Webb had sincere feelings of love and respect for his young counterpart. Accounts vary on the subject of Chick adopting Ella. Some say yes while others quote Chick as claiming it was all for the press. Regardless, the two were very close, supportive and loving of one another.

Cover 1939 Gretsch Catalogue

Still with a passion for drums, in 1938 Chick accepted an endorsement offer from the Gretsch Drum Company to play their new Gretsch Gladstone drums. A special finish was designed exclusively for Chick that consisted of "White Oriental Pearl with Green Sparkle Baby Chicks Strolling Around the Circumference."[8] This covered all five drums, a (still large) 14 by 28 inch bass drum, a 9 by 13 inch tom tom on his left, 16 by 14 inch floor tom on his right, both with wooden hoops, and 6 ½ by 14 inch snare drum. It was the snare drum that was again an innovative design. At the time, drumheads were natural calf skin (rather than plastic used today). These natural skins were subject to climatic conditions and very often required tensioning. Gladstone's design allowed the player to adjust the tension of both the top and bottom snare heads from the top tension rods, thus the drum did not need to be turned over to adjust the bottom head tension. Chick, like drummers today, was an equipment freak and found this innovative design appealing. While his cymbal set up remained the same, Zildjian was using Chick in their advertising. The set was still mounted on the Premier rolling console but now fitted with a clear Plexiglas trap table, another invention of Gladstone "which covers the drummers whole outfit but does not conceal it from the audience. Audiences are very curious about drummers and their gadgets. They like to see everything, fascinated by the drummer's equipment and performance."[9] In the April 1939 issue of *Metronome*, Gretsch Drums ran a full-page ad for their Gretsch Gladstone drums featuring Chick Webb. "When Gretsch printed their first catalogue that included Gretsch-Gladstone drums in 1939, Chick Webb was prominently pictured on the cover with his set. Sharing the cover is Bernie Mattinson, a drummer also well-known for his technique. A comparison of the two photographs is revealing. While Mattinson has the appearance and composure of a 'society drummer,' the 'King of Drums' as Chick Webb was known, appears to be in ecstasy behind his set of Gretsch-Gladstones. With his head rolled back and arms flailing, Chick has all the appearance of 'true hippness.'"[10]

The Webb group went on the road again taking a thirteen-week engagement at the Flamingo Room of Levaggi's Restaurant in Boston. March 1938 *Metronome*, praised the performance with, "Webb Slays 'Em In Boston, The old Beantown is writhing from its first concentrated dose of real, colored swing in many a

[8] Jon Cohan, *Star Sets*, (Milwaukee: Hal Leonard, 1995).

[9] No author credited, "Gladstone Invents Gadgets While Drumming," *Metronome*, September 1937.

[10] Chet Falzerano, *Gretsch Drums, The Legacy of "That Great Gretsch Sound,"* (Fullerton, CA, Centerstream Publishing, 1995).

Gretsch Gladstone Drum Ad, Metronome Magazine, April 1939

moon. Chick Webb's Chicks at Levaggi's are tossing the potent shots that's got the cats up here chasing the chicks more than ever. The band has just been renewed for another four weeks, meaning that it'll be here till April 6th – at least!"[11] In truth, it was renewed till May 2. "Artie Shaw, 'I remember when my band was taking form in Boston in 1938, he was playing at Levaggi's. Now and then he would come by and listen to the band. During one of the rehearsals, he sat very quietly in the dimly-lit cellar, chewing gum, obviously deep in thought. When we got finished, he came over to me and said: "You know somethin', man? Some day I'm gonna be walkin' up the street and you gonna be comin' down the other way, and we gonna pass each other and I'm gonna say, 'Hello, best white band in the worl'' and you gonna say, 'Hello, best colored band in the worl'' – you know that?" And he gravely shook hands with me on that statement, almost as if we were entering into a solemn pact – and in a way, I suppose we actually were.'"[12] The intense schedule was beginning to catch up with Webb's disability and frailty. He was admitted to a hospital on April 4 for two weeks, requiring a replacement at Levaggi's. "Webb rarely took a breather. He didn't want to be known as sickly, so he would keep going. His loyalty to his musicians also made it impossible for him to ease up. He seemed to sense that a lot had to be accomplished before the last chorus. Despite the fatigue and pain, he accepted a tiring schedule of theatre, ballroom, and club dates in New York and on the road."[13] Indeed when the Levaggi's gig ended, Chick and the band were immediately back in the Decca studios. Two cuts that day defined Chick Webb, both arranged by Van Alexander. Van Alexander, "one day I got to Boston, Ella says to me, 'I got a great idea for a song. Why don't you try to work up something on the old nursery rhyme *A-Tisket, A-Tasket?*' And I said, 'Gee, that is a great idea, Ella, lemme think about it.' Well Chick, as I said, had given me assignments for the following two weeks -- that would be six tunes -- and so I just didn't have time to think about *A-Tisket, A-Tasket*. She said, 'Did you think about [it]?' I said, 'I thought about it, Ella, but I just didn't have the time.' The following week, the same thing happened, I didn't get to it, and this time, Ella got a little testy (which she'd never done). She said, 'Well, look, if you don't want to do it, I'll ask Edgar (Sampson) to do it, 'cause I think it's too good an idea to... 'Hold the phone! (I said) I'll get to it next week, I promise ya.' Now, you gotta realize, the old nursery rhyme *A-Tisket, A-Tasket* was in [the] public domain. There was never really a song, it was just a little rhythm thing that the kids used to sing. What I did was to put it into form, a 32-bar song. I put the release, the bridge to it, and all the novelty things to it ('Was it red? No-no, no-no. Was it blue?' and so forth). And I brought it up to Boston, and Ella and I went over it and she changed a lot of the

Decca Records "A-Tisket A-Tasket," May 1938

Van Alexander, Metronome Magazine, Sept. 1937

[11] No author credited, "Webb Slays 'Em In Boston," *Metronome*, March 1938.
[12] Burt Korall, *Drummin' Men* (New York: Schirmer Books, 1990).
[13] Ibid.

words. I had written, in the middle part, I said [sings] 'She was walkin' on down the avenue, without a single thing to do,' and Ella said, 'Let's say she was *truckin'* on down the avenue. Not walkin', *truckin'*, 'cause that was a big word in those days, you know. So I said, 'Yes, great!' And she changed a few other lyrics also. Well, they put it on the air that night, and somebody telephoned Robbins Music in New York and asked them to take [an acetate] off the air. And they did, and they got excited about it, and two weeks later, [the band] went to New York, to Decca Records, and recorded it -- on my birthday, incidentally -- May 2nd, 1938. It was a big hit that summer, and on the Lucky Strike 'Hit Parade,' which was the big radio program in those days, it stayed #1 for 19 weeks."[14] The other cut recorded May 2 was "Liza," another classic Webb "Bullet" that he used to take down his band battle opponents. Aside from "Harlem Congo," "Liza" is the only other studio recorded platform of Webb's dexterity. Burt Korall, "A well-balanced piece in a medium tempo, it features some of Webb's best work on record. From the twenty-four bar opening solo through the various eight, four, and two-bar breaks, he demonstrated space, heat, and musicality. Webb serves the band particularly well, providing supportive figures and bass drum 'shots' to swing things along. Balance and a sense of control are the hallmarks of the recording. Only once does he briefly lose hold of things; his chops fail and he bunches up some triplets, affecting the solo flow."[15] Chick also bunched up some triplets at the end of his solo on "Undecided" which resulted in a misguided entrance for Ella and the band. "Buddy Rich, 'Chick wasn't perfect. Though fast and terribly talented, he didn't have a stable, well-rounded technique. He was a little like a pitcher who can throw a ball 100 miles an hour but doesn't have the discipline to win all the time. Chick's dexterity and speed didn't work for him as well as they might have. They didn't always take him where he wanted to go. A drummer as natural and gifted as Chick should have been able to exercise a bit more control over what he played."[16] Not to follow the typical historian path of concentrating on the negative performances, if you want to hear Webb at his supreme best, find the First Time Records cut of "Wild Irish Rose." This was a live recording (thus not listed in the discography) of a radio broadcast from The Southland Café in Boston May 4, 1939 (only 6 weeks before Chick's death). After four bars of a medium swing opening, Webb lights a fire under the band with a four bar quick send-off, driving the band (and the crowd) into a frenzy. The band then

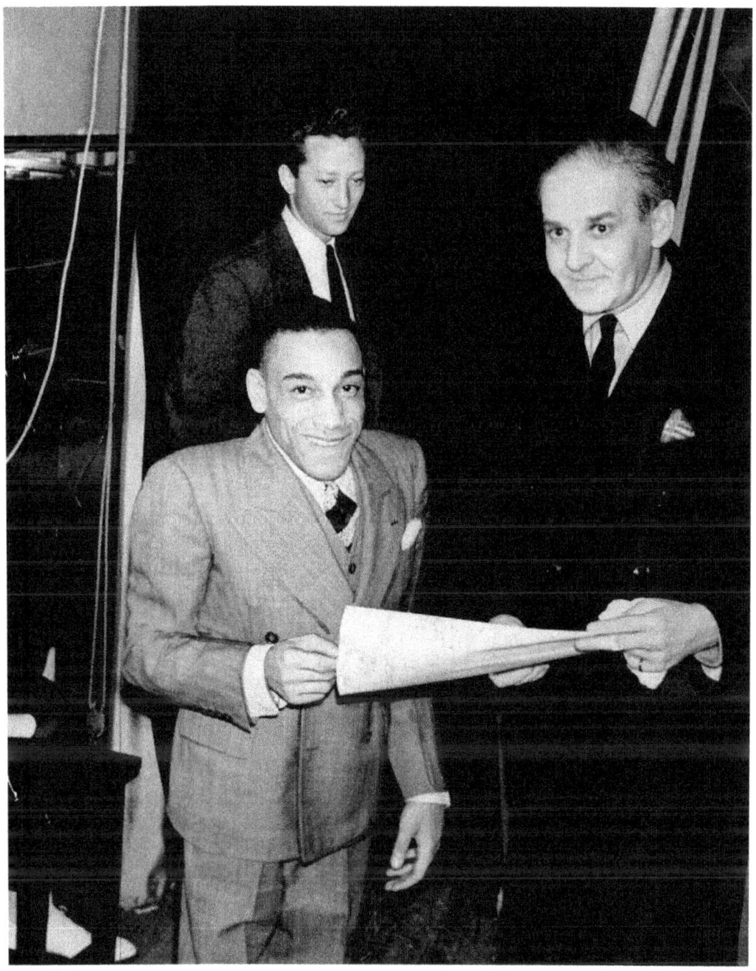

WEBB AND WALTER WINCHELL RECEIVING HONORARY DEGREES

[14] Christopher Popa "CHICK WEBB 'Stompin' At the Savoy'" (http://www.bigbandlibrary.com/chickwebb.html 2004).

[15] Burt Korall, *Drummin' Men* (New York: Schirmer Books, 1990).

[16] Ibid.

"CARNIVAL OF SWING" RANDALL'S ISLAND STADIUM, NEW YORK

drifts back into a slumbering tempo two more times only to have Chick kick them into high gear again. If ever there was an example of what the Savoy performances might have been like, this is it. With "A-Tisket, A-Tasket" Ella Fitzgerald and Chick Webb became national celebrities. Both had realized their dreams. Chick was receiving press accolades as well. This photo appeared in the *Baltimore Afro American* with the caption "Chick Webb is shown with Walter Winchell, just after he received an M.D. degree (Master of Drums) from the senior class of New York University. Winchell, famous New York columnist, and radio and screen star, was also awarded a degree by the class. A few months ago Chick got an M.S. (Master of Swing) degree from a fraternity in Boston University."[17] The subsequent schedule became more frenetic. The studio demanded more hits. Promoters queued to fill Chick's appearance schedule. And Chick's health worsened. Several times he had to ask his friends Sid Catlett, Jesse Price, Kaiser Marshall, and Bill Beason to fill in for him. But when asked to perform May 29 at the Martin Block "Carnival Of Swing" at Randall's Island Stadium, a benefit for unemployed musicians, Chick unselfishly rallied to the cause. Twenty-six bands played to a capacity crowd of 25,000 while WNEW broadcast the seven-hour event live. On July 31, Webb scheduled another (and final) band battle while on the road at the Savoy Ballroom in Chicago against Horace Henderson with Alvin Burroughs on drums. To the delight of concert organizers, Ella and Webb's popularity meant capacity crowds at their venues. The Webb/Horace Henderson Battle drew 6,000 eager patrons when 4,000 was considered a good night at the South Side of Chicago landmark. Then in September, Chick broke a five-year attendance record at the Paramount Theatre in New York. Only two other black bands had played the Paramount, Cab Calloway and Louis Armstrong. Webb returned to the Paramount in September, then in October he broke Benny Goodman's record at the Regal Theatre in Chicago. In November, Ella and Chick performed at the all-white Coconut Grove of the Park Central Hotel in downtown Manhattan. Sadly, "At the Paramount Theatre, he didn't have the strength to walk off the bandstand himself and had to be carried by his valet and bodyguard Joe Saunders."[18] This image of Chick at the Paramount is the last known photograph of him performing. Amongst their busy performance schedule, the Webb organization recorded five more sessions at Decca to finish out the year.

CHICK WEBB PERFORMING AT THE PARAMOUNT THEATRE, NYC JUST BEFORE HIS DEATH.

[17] No author credited, *Baltimore Afro American*, June 18, 1938.

[18] Burt Korall, *Drummin' Men* (New York: Schirmer Books, 1990).

It's Lots of Fun to PLAY the DRUMS

...and EASY, too!

CHICK WEBB
King of the Drums

Step out in front! Be entertaining . . . popular . . . sought-after by friends. Start to play a GRETSCH DRUM. Begin a BIG MONEY career—be an ace drummer like Chick Webb, "The King of the Drums". Chick and thousands of others have won success on radio, stage and screen using GRETSCH equipment. EASY TO PLAY—no difficult lessons. Buy GRETSCH DRUMS, on NEW EASY-PAYMENT plan.

Send penny postcard for FREE DRUM catalogue and full information about EASY-PAYMENT plan and FREE TRIAL through your GRETSCH dealer. Address Dept. PS 60

EASY TO PLAY ★ EASY TO PAY

The FRED. GRETSCH MFG. CO.
Musical Instrument Makers Since 1883
60 BROADWAY, BROOKLYN, N. Y.

GRETSCH also offers SUPER VALUES in Guitars, Saxophones, Trumpets, Trombones, Accordions. Send for FREE catalogue. Mention instrument.

FINALE

When the Park Central engagement ended in January, Chick was back on the road with a grueling tour schedule. More and more his failing health required him to rest and find a substitute for a performance. Equally, the recording sessions were busy albeit titles like "Chew Chew Chew (Your Bubble Gum)" and "Coochi-Coochi-Coo." Regardless, the public couldn't get enough and the Webb organization was enjoying unprecedented popularity. In April Chick was admitted to Johns Hopkins Hospital in Baltimore for treatment. Fluid was accumulating in his back and doctors recommended it be removed. "Helen Oakley Dance. 'He was frightened of hospitals; he figured, like a lot of people, that if he went in he might never come out.'"[1] Unfortunately the operation was unsuccessful and his condition worsened. After being discharged from the hospital, Webb returned to another Park Central engagement followed by a date at the Southland Café in Boston. One-nighters continued including playing two cruises (8:45PM and 12:30AM) June 3 on the S.S. Potomac in Washington, DC. Kaiser Marshall took over for Chick who fell ill after the first cruise, returning to Johns Hopkins for further treatment. Teddy McRae, "He was driving back to Baltimore and he was telling me, 'Anything happen to me…take care of Ella. Don't let the guys mess up, just take care of Ella.' I said, 'Ah, man, come on, you're going to be all right.' He said, 'Nah, I got to take care of business. Take care of Ella.' I say, 'OK, I'll see you in Florida in four or five days.' 'I'll be down there' said Webb."[2] "Helen Oakley Dance, 'He was at death's door for two or three days at Johns Hopkins Hospital in Baltimore and was resisting it bravely until, in the end, he knew he had to go. It was just astonishing. There he was propped up on his pillows and he suddenly said, "I'm sorry, but I gotta go." And he died right then and there."[3] Ella and the Chick Webb Orchestra were performing in Montgomery,

CHICK WEBB "THE KING OF THE DRUMS"

B. Goodman Signs Fletcher and Sepia Songstress

FIRST in NEWS and PICTURES

Harlem Jazz

10c PER COPY

The Negro Musician's Own Monthly Newspaper

Chick Webb Dies; Band Carries On

Hawkins To Form U. S. Ork

The King Is Dead

Death A Shock To Band World

Fletcher Goes To Goodman

"CHICK WEBB DIES" HARLEM JAZZ

[1] Burt Korall, *Drummin' Men* (New York: Schirmer Books, 1990).
[2] Stuart Nicholson, *Ella Fitzgerald* (London: Victor Gollancz, 1993).
[3] Burt Korall, Drummin' Men (New York: Schirmer Books, 1990).

CROWD OUTSIDE WATERS AME CHURCH, BALTIMORE, MD

AL when they got word of the news and immediately played "Taps," followed by "My Buddy." The remainder of the tour was cancelled. "Teddy McRae, 'We returned the next day – June 17 – to Baltimore for the funeral. People came from all over. I remember the body was laid out in his home on the first floor. People kept coming through the little parlor and moving out into the street. The funeral was one of the largest ever held in Baltimore. People lined the rooftops and filled the streets. You couldn't get near the Church. An amazing thing happened – what I call a shower of blessing. Before they brought the body out of Waters AME Church, it rained like cats and dogs. And just about two or three minutes before the funeral was over, it stopped. I don't know where the rain came from. It had been a hot sunny day. The crowds of people didn't move. Before you knew it, the sun was shining again.' Van Alexander, ' I drove in from New York. It was impossible to get to the church without the help from the police. They moved me through the crowds. That sad occasion left me with so many memories – kids and grown-ups sitting on top of trolley cars, Ella singing "My Buddy" in the church, Teddy McRae playing a tenor solo ("The End Of A Perfect Day"). So many famous musicians and entertainers were there to say goodbye.'"[4]

WEBB'S TOMBSTONE, BALTIMORE, MD

Webb being cut down at such an early age with comparatively few years in his struggle for acceptance makes almost a forgotten story from the past. Since the limitations of recording equipment only imply his true greatness, we have only the first hand personal accounts of those who witnessed his extraordinary faculty behind a drumset. Buddy Rich, the "World's Greatest Drummer" astutely noted, "You know, only about a half-dozen of the top drummers since then, including today's so-called 'great' drummers, have anything resembling what he had. If he were alive now, I think most drummers would be running around trying to figure out why they decided to play drums. That's how good he was.'[5] If only he had been given the years of Ella, Sinatra, Armstrong, his legacy and this account would be much richer.

[4] Ibid.

[5] Ibid.

CODA

For many years I searched for Chick Webb's original drum set only to come up empty handed. I decided to recreate the set using drums from the era. This article was published in the *Classic Drummer Magazine* Summer Edition 2014.

Chick Webb Tribute Set by Chet Falzerano

Reproduction of Chick Webb's Set by the author.

Gretsch Gladstone snare drum, Tucson Guitar Center

"The Project of a Lifetime For the Right Buyer"...those were the words of the eBay seller for a Premier 'Gigster' set that is literally the foundation of this 'project of a lifetime' endeavor. My collecting to this point did not include any 'creative' efforts. That is, I have always collected vintage drums and restored them, if needed. This time I went beyond restoration. I invented. The project began with the purchase of a Gretsch Gladstone 3-way snare that a previous owner had stripped off its finish and painted flat black. I was carefully weighing my options for a proper 'period correct' finish when it occurred to me that it was the perfect candidate for a Chick Webb Gretsch Gladstone replica snare drum. In Webb's short lifetime (he died in 1939, four months after his 30th birthday) he garnered probably more accolades then any other drummer, including from Buddy Rich. Not known to be effusive in his opinions, Rich is quoted in Burt Korall's *Drummin' Men*, "If he were alive now, I think most drummers would be running around trying to figure out why they decided to play drums. That's how good he was. Gene [Krupa] got to the heart of the matter when he said, after the Goodman-Webb band battle at the Savoy in '37, 'I've never been cut by a better man.'" I have searched my entire collecting career for Webb's original Gretsch Gladstone 'Chick' set. Webb was one of the first endorsers of Gretsch Gladstone drums and Gretsch built a custom set in white oriental pearl with green sparkle 'Chicks' for him. Since I could not find the original, I thought, why not recreate the snare drum? Many folks helped in this effort but it was my wife Judith who deserves the most credit for this project. As a cellist in the Mainz Germany Symphony one would think she would be the least likely candidate for drum restoration…au contraire…from her masterful work cutting out the green sparkle chicks, to tucking new heads, to painting the 'Chick' caricature on the resonator bass drum head, Judith was a godsend. Thankfully, others chimed-in as well: Mike Kaskell alerted me of the Guitar Center listing of the Gretsch Gladstone snare, Harry Cangany found the source for the 'Chick' image, Jon Cohan the color configuration of the 'Chick' Gretsch Gladstones ('White Oriental Pearl with Green Sparkle Baby Chicks Strolling Around the Circumference', *Star Sets* by Jon Cohan), Brooks Tegler offered endless advice and rare vintage pearl covering and parts, the list goes on and on.

Chick's Gretsch Gladstone "Chick" Set

Gretsch Gladstone Snare Drum Arrives

When the snare arrived, it turned out to be better than I expected. Fortunately, the drum was original (aside from the refinish) lacking only original snare wires and calf heads (both of which I had). The drum has features I have not seen before in other Gretsch Gladstones. The tone control incorporates an adjustable stop inside the drum enabling a variable pressure of the dampening pads against the top head. The other features are cosmetic: a 'Gretsch Gladstone' logo stamped on the throw off arm and identification stamps on the three-way key: "Batter, Snare, Both." As you may be aware, the three-way Gladstone patent allows tensioning of the batter,

Reproduction of Webb's Gretsch Gladstone Snare Drum

snare, and both heads, all from the top tension rods. The unusual features incorporated in this snare may have been dropped from later production models as a cost-saving measure. The Gretsch-Gladstone was the most expensive snare produced at the time. William F. Ludwig, Jr. recalls, "I remember Gretsch reserving a suite at the Sherman Hotel (in Chicago) and inviting all the Chicago drummers to see the marvelous Gladstone drum. The drum sold for $100, which was ridiculous in those days. Our top of the line drum was $35." As ridiculous as it may have seemed, Gretsch-Gladstone drums were being used by prominent drummers of the day. Paramount among this group was the inimitable 'Chick' Webb. This drum, otherwise, is your basic 6 1/2 by 14 inch 3-way drum from the mid 1930's, 3-ply maple shell with 3-ply reinforcement rings, a Gretsch Gladstone throw off and 'Ring Eliminator' (tone control). A previous owner moved the Gretsch Gladstone badge from its original position above the throw off to the panel adjacent to the throw off, an easy fix.

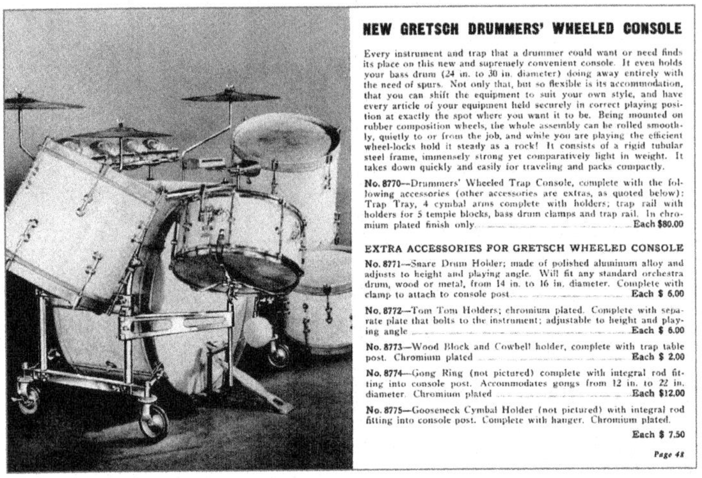

NEW GRETSCH DRUMMERS' WHEELED CONSOLE

Every instrument and trap that a drummer could want or need finds its place on this new and supremely convenient console. It even holds your bass drum (24 in. to 30 in. diameter) doing away entirely with the need of spurs. Not only that, but so flexible is its accommodation, that you can shift the equipment to suit your own style, and have every article of your equipment held securely in correct playing position at exactly the spot where you want it to be. Being mounted on rubber composition wheels, the whole assembly can be rolled smoothly, quietly to or from the job, and while you are playing the efficient wheel-locks hold it steady as a rock! It consists of a rigid tubular steel frame, immensely strong yet comparatively light in weight. It takes down quickly and easily for traveling and packs compactly.

No. 8770—Drummers' Wheeled Trap Console, complete with the following accessories (other accessories are extras, as quoted below): Trap Tray, 4 cymbal arms complete with holders; trap rail with holders for 5 temple blocks, bass drum clamps and trap rail. In chromium plated finish only .... **Each $80.00**

EXTRA ACCESSORIES FOR GRETSCH WHEELED CONSOLE

No. 8771—Snare Drum Holder; made of polished aluminum alloy and adjusts to height and playing angle. Will fit any standard orchestra drum, wood or metal, from 14 in. to 16 in. diameter. Complete with clamp to attach to console post .... **Each $ 6.00**

No. 8772—Tom Tom Holders; chromium plated. Complete with separate plate that bolts to the instrument; adjustable to height and playing angle .... **Each $ 6.00**

No. 8773—Wood Block and Cowbell holder, complete with trap table post. Chromium plated .... **Each $ 2.00**

No. 8774—Gong Ring (not pictured) complete with integral rod fitting into console post. Accommodates gongs from 12 in. to 22 in. diameter. Chromium plated .... **Each $12.00**

No. 8775—Gooseneck Cymbal Holder (not pictured) with integral rod fitting into console post. Complete with hanger. Chromium plated. **Each $ 7.50**

Page 48

GRETSCH WHEELED CONSOLE

As work slowly progressed on the snare drum I posted a 'progress report' on the Billy Gladstone Facebook page www.facebook.com/billy.gladstone. I not only received much admiration of the project but some great advice and help. Early on, I was encouraged to replicate the entire Chick Webb Gretsch Gladstone set. 'Easy for you to say!' I thought. Just try to find a set of Gretsch Gladstones, especially with a custom 16 X 14 floor tom that Webb obviously preferred. Then there's the console…Chick's set was mounted on a New Gretsch Drummers' Wheeled Console with those iconic gooseneck cymbal arms. Gretsch was importing these consoles from Premier Drums in the UK. Premier's name for this model was 'Swingster Console.' I found a Swingster console for sale in the UK but with a hefty price tag of $1200. Still, there was the issue of finding the Gretsch Gladstone drums. Putting a set together with new shells and hardware didn't appeal to me so I resigned myself to being content with just the snare drum. After applying Tegler's period correct white oriental pearl and green sparkle for the 'Chicks,' the finishing touch of the snare drum is an engraved plaque commemorating Webb's illustrious albeit short career. The Chick Webb Orchestra was the house band at the Savoy Ballroom located at 596 Lenox Avenue in Harlem. There, Webb earned the title of the 'King of the Drums' after he routed The Benny Goodman Orchestra in a Battle of the Bands in 1937. It is a well-known fact that Benny Goodman, known internationally as the 'King of Swing' was summarily out-swung by Chick Webb and his orchestra. If you have the opportunity to view the documentary "The Savoy King, Chick Webb and the Music That Changed America," I highly recommend it. At times redundant, it nevertheless chronicles the life of the great Chick Webb. http://savoyking.com/.

COMMEMORATIVE PLAQUE

GOODMAN/WEBB BATTLE OF THE BANDS

WEBB'S FRANK WOLF DRUM SET

I have always admired Webb's set prior to his endorsement with Gretsch Gladstone, especially the 'Chick' caricature logo on the front of the bass drum. It was a simpler set up with an earlier version of the 'Swingster' console, but only one mounted tom on his right. I assumed it was a Gretsch set as, early on, Gretsch used a similar box-like lug. This was also confirmed by Mel Torme's foreword to Burt Korall's book *Drummin' Men*, "and the elaborate caricature gracing the head of Chick Webb's Gretsch bass drum." Then I received a message from Brooks Tegler. "I was studying this set and noticed the snare drum had staggered lugs. Did Gretsch offer a snare drum like this?" Careful inspection of the photo revealed the snare was a "Frank Wolf 2 to 1 Tension Snare Drum." In 1910, Wolf opened a drum store on 48th Street in New York City. The back room of the store revealed a small assembly plant that boasted several innovative drum designs. Paramount among those was this "2 to 1" snare with 12 lugs on top and 6 on the bottom. The theory was, the top head of a snare requires considerably more tension than the bottom. With a 'more is better' concept, Wolf designed a drum that would presumably distribute this tension evenly.

FRANK WOLF DRUMMERS SUPPLY

Brook's discovery set me on a new path, especially when this Premier 'Gigster' Console Kit was posted on eBay/UK. The Gigster console was Premier's second level console with all the features of the Swingster but with a frame made of angle iron rather than tubes. Still, it caught my eye with those incredible gooseneck cymbal arms and correct 28 inch bass drum. It was truly a 'Time Capsule' find by the eBay lister:

EBAY PREMIER DRUM SET

"The kit belongs to two delightful sisters who have had it stored since emptying their late father's home. He bought the kit new 'a couple of years before the war' (World War II). I was buying books from the family and spotted the drum cases in the self-store unit we were working in. Knowing something of drums I am selling the kit on their behalf."

I say "Time Capsule" in that this Premier Gigster Kit included everything as listed in the 1937 Premier catalogue, down to the original Premier 'C' drumsticks, which hardly show wear. It was as if the father bought the set in '37, played it a few times, got distracted by the war, cased them up and never touched them again. Unfortunately, a family of woodworms moved in to the storage unit as well. The bass drum was riddled with tiny holes. The lister disclosed:

"The bass drum shell is beyond help. It is riddled with woodworm, which I have treated, but it's no good. It's paper thin in places. After I took the pictures in the garden, where I was cleaning the drum, two of the bass drum lugs came off in my hands complete with bits of shell! The hoops I think are re-usable. A new shell can be easily made and I have ALL the fittings to put onto it. Badge, lugs, tension rods etc. The finish is easy as it's black paint! The calf heads are probably also re-usable - there are very small areas where the woodworm attempted a change of diet. I don't think they liked old calf."

"PET FARM"

"A new shell can be easily made"?...a 28 inch shell?...I think not. Still, I put the set on my watch list and kept a close eye as the price slowly crept upward. I thought, if the Swingster console alone is going for $1200, I'll wait and 'snipe' a bid of $900 in the last seconds. 28 inch bass drums can be had inexpensively and all the other bits and pieces were included with set, including a 12" Constantinople K splash cymbal. Fortunately, my bid prevailed and I got the set for $700.

When the set arrived the bass drum immediately went to the basement. No sense risking other instruments or furniture to the woodworm appetite. I began by polishing the hardware. Everything you have heard about the superiority of Premier's chrome plating is absolutely true. After probably sitting untouched for 75 years, the console and various hardware pieces polished up beautifully. The temple blocks, so often found with the lacquer chipped off, were also in excellent condition. The 12 inch Constantinople K is the best splash I have had the pleasure of owning. Paired with a 13 inch Constantinople K Splash, a 15 inch Su Chou China, and a pair of paper thin 12 inch Avedis Zildjian Hi Hats and Chick's cymbal setup is complete.

I was not willing to give up on the bass drum. It has always given me great pleasure to save some poor ol' relic from the dustbin. Frankly though, I am surprised the drum made it through the shipping process. The seller packed it carefully but the shell was so fragile, I wasn't sure it could be saved. Two of the lugs had been snapped off leaving gaping holes. When I posted the set on Facebook, one comment was "Isn't that the drum that came with a free pet farm?" All joking aside, the woodworms were voracious, albeit lazy. Fortunately the wood glue rings inside held most of their integrity. Though the seller claimed he treated the shell with chemicals, I applied another strong treatment. Not trusting that the chemical would soak through the calfskin to the wood flesh hoops, I pulled the heads off the hoops before I treated them. After I was sure the prior tenants were gone, my plan was to apply a veneer ply inside the drum with reinforcement panels where

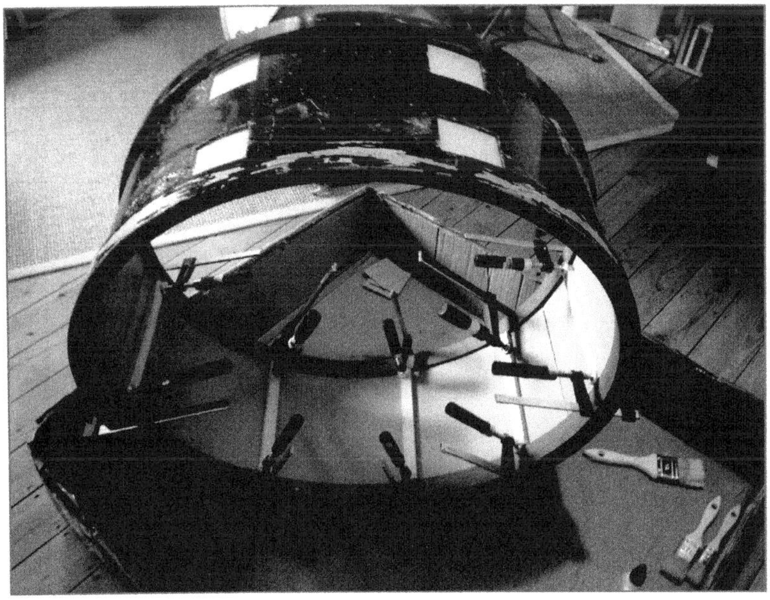

LAMINATE

the lugs had broken away from the shell. With a pearl wrap outside, I hoped the shell could be saved. Let's just say the inner ply is a bit more porous than usual. Off I go to the local woodshop specializing in veneers. I was thinking of a veneer of birch, the same wood as the other plies of the bass drum. The owner of the wood shop said, "As you like, but Masonite would be better, more uniform and bendable." Who am I to argue with the expert? The ply glued in easily, as well the patches for the rotted lug holes. A wrap of green sparkle outside and the bass drum is as good as new. Amazingly, I found a new supply of green sparkle that matched Tegler's vintage pearl used for the snare drum.

Why green sparkle, you ask? As I noted earlier, I have always been partial to Webb's Frank Wolf set because of the caricature on the bass drum. Of course the Gretsch Gladstone set had the 'Chick' appliqués (not 'inlays') but the painted crown on the Gretsch bass drum head just doesn't compare with the cartoon caricature of Webb on the Wolf set. Though I found the pearl color configuration of the Gretsch Gladstone Chick set in Jon Cohan's *Star Sets* book, no record exists of the sparkle color of the Wolf set. I love green sparkle and maybe this was a leading question, but I asked Cohan, "Since the Chicks on the Gretsch Gladstone set are green sparkle, wouldn't you think the Wolf set was green sparkle too?" Jon's reply was "Can't say for sure, Chet, but it seems probable." Good enough for me...green sparkle it is! Inlays had to be cut in the hoops and the bass drum is complete.

CARICATURE BASS DRUM PAINTING

The remaining elements were the mounted tom and a high hat stand, both supplied by Brooks Tegler. This guy is amazing, not just because he is an incredible player, but for his endless stash of vintage drums and parts, and his knowledge. If he doesn't know the answer of a vintage drum question, he will find one and you can bet it will be correct. I said I needed a Walberg and Auge 501 Hi Hat stand. He asked "Which one?' Knowing full well

GREEN SPARKLE COVERING

he knew something I didn't, I sent him a picture of Chick's set. "Oh I have one of those I can spare you." Curiosity got the best of me and I said, "I only know of one." "The picture you sent me is the earlier version without the 'Y' shaped flange at the front of the footboard" he replied. Not to sound stupid I said "Oh, right. I also need a 12 X 14 tom." He replied, "I have a period correct (late 30's) Slingerland, but since you will be recovering it, I'd like to keep the black diamond pearl wrap" (he has a collection of vintage wraps too). I did my best duplicating Webb's tack bottom tom with no less than 220 tacks. Even the top head was tacked on to the wood counter hoop (no flesh hoop).

BOY TEN HOVE

I met up with Brooks while he was on tour here in Germany. As I said, what a player! Brooks has shared the stage with many great jazz artists. He will laugh when he reads this but as an old blues drummer, I was most impressed when he told me he had a gig with Muddy Waters. He instinctively knew where I wanted the conversation to go. "You know about the caricature on the bass drum head, right? (long pause on my part) That was done by Boy ten Hove, a little known Dutch artist of famous 30's jazz greats. He also did the bass drum head on Jimmy Crawford's drum (Jimmy Lunceford's Band)." Brooks had a book published about Ten Hove's caricatures aptly named *Boy ten Hove's caricatures* by Ate van Delden…fascinating reading.

The final element was painting the Webb caricature on the bass drum resonator head. Again my wife Judith steps in. She experimented with several mediums, acrylic, oil base paint, charcoal, and ink. It was ink that eventually won out. Coincidentally, Boy ten Hove's original works, according to the book, were done in ink and pencil. The original black and white Hove drawing of Chick Webb did not include a crown. As noted on page 331 of *Boy ten Hove's caricatures*, "This drawing was also used to promote dances at the Savoy Ballroom" and indeed is included in the poster promoting the Chick Webb/Count Basie Battle of the Bands January 16, 1938. Note the caption "The King of the Drums" which Webb presumably earned after he out-swung "The King of Swing" Benny Goodman one year earlier. As I said, there are no color photographs of Webb's sets. I elected to colorize the crown, as was also the choice for this album jacket. It is a distinct possibility that when the crown was added to the Ten Hove caricature on the front of Webb's bass drum that colors were present. I think Judith did a remarkable job recreating Boy's work.

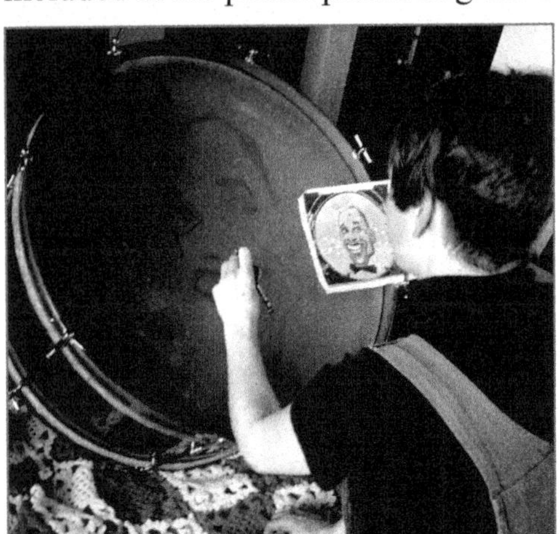

JUDITH RENDERING

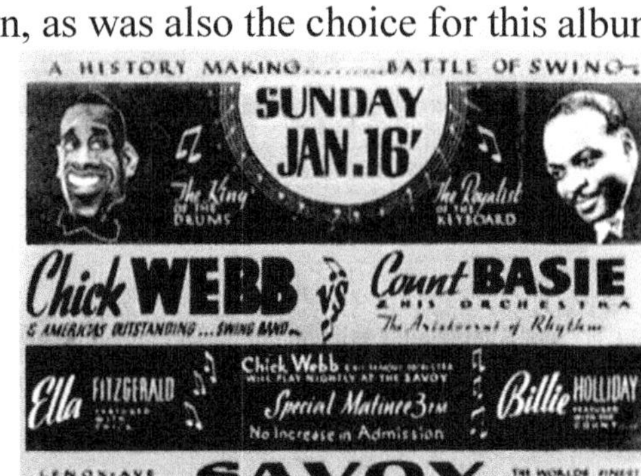

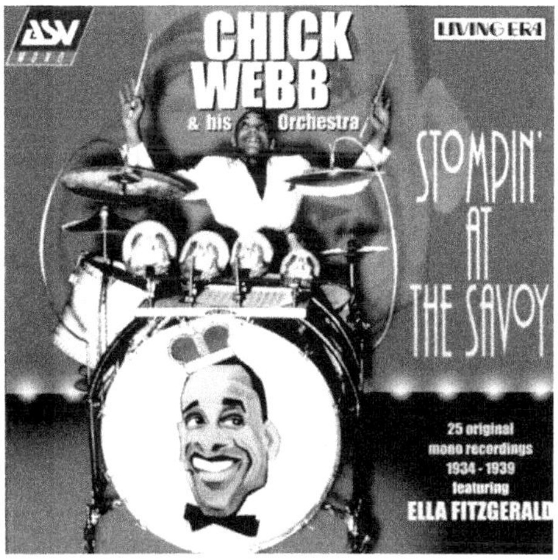

CROWN

So here is my creation, the Chick Webb Tribute set…not the Gretsch Gladstone 'Chick' set, nor the Frank Wolf set, but a hybrid of the two. Normally I am quite anal about vintage drum restoration and would never think of assembling a mishmash of pieces. I like to think of this creative effort as the imaginary set Chick played before he got his Gretsch Gladstone endorsement. You know he received the Gretsch Gladstone snare first. Could you resist trying your new snare with your old set?

……………………………………………………………………………………

COMPLETE SET

6 ½ x 14 Gretsch Gladstone Snare ca 1937 Refinished in White Oriental Pearl with Green Sparkle Chicks (original finish unknown)

Premier Gigster Console Kit ca 1937, 12 x 28 Premier Bass Drum Refinished in Green Sparkle (originally ebony lacquer), Two Maxi Cymbal Arms, Four Temple Blocks, Cow Bell, Woodblock, Deluxe Express Bass Drum Pedal, Bass Drum Damper, Bi-fold Snare Stand

12 x 14 Slingerland Tom ca 1939 Refinished in Green Sparkle (originally black diamond pearl)

Walberg & Auge #501 Hi Hat

12" A Zildjian Paper Thin Hi Hat Cymbals
12" Constantinople K Zildjian Paper Thin Splash
13" Constantinople K Zildjian Paper Thin Splash
15" Su Chou China
Billy Gladstone Hand Sock Cymbals

Chet Falzerano is the author of two other Centerstream Publications:
Gretsch Drums The Legacy of "That Great Gretsch Sound" and *Billy Gladstone.*

www.centerstream-usa.com

Falzerano also co-authored chapters in the Centerstream publication *Guide to Vintage Drums* by John Aldridge and the Hal Leonard publication, *Star Sets* by Jon Cohan. Falzerano has been published in the following magazines: *DRUM!, Classic Drummer, Modern Drummer, Percussive Notes, North South Traders CIVIL War*, and *Not So Modern Drummer*.

BATTLE OF THE BANDS

DATE	OPPOSING ORCHESTRA	DRUMMER	LOCATION
May 15, 1927	King Oliver's Dixie Syncopators	Paul Barbarin	Savoy Ballroom, Harlem, NY
	Fletcher Henderson's Roseland Orchestra	Kaiser Marshall	
	Fess Williams' Royal Flush Orchestra	Ralph Bedell	
May 6, 1928	Lloyd Scott & His Symphonic Syncopators	Lloyd Scott	Savoy Ballroom, Harlem, NY
	Fess Williams' Royal Flush Orchestra	Ralph Bedell	
	Alex Jackson's Plantation Orchestra	Dick Ward	
	Charlie Johnson's Paradise Orchestra	George Stafford	
May 14,1930	Cab Calloway and the Missourians	Leroy Maxey	Savoy Ballroom, Harlem, NY
	Duke Ellington Orchestra	Sonny Greer	
	Cecil Scott and his Bright Boys	Arnold Bolden	
	Lockwood Lewis Orchestra	?	
Feb. 2, 1935	Willie Bryant and His Orchestra	Cozy Cole	Savoy Ballroom, Harlem, NY
Apr. 24, 1935	Glen Gray's Casa Loma Orchestra	Tony Briglia	Savoy Ballroom, Harlem, NY
Jul. 28, 1935	Julie Wintz Palisades Band	George Zimmer	Palisades Amusement Park, Fort Lee, NJ
Oct. 14, 1935	Buddy Johnson	?	Strand Theatre, Baltimore, MD
Oct. 27, 1935	Ruth Ellington Orchestra	?	Cotton Club, Nashville, TN
Nov. 3, 1935	Jimmy Noone Orchestra	Johnny Wells	Savoy Ballroom, Chicago, IL
Jun. 12, 1936	Fletcher Henderson Orchestra	Kaiser Marshall	8th Regiment Armory, Chicago, IL
	Erskine Tate	Jimmie Bertrand	
	Don Redman	Manzie Johnson	
Dec. 13, 1936	Tommy Dorsey Orchestra	Dave Tough	Savoy Ballroom, Harlem, NY
Feb. 28, 1937	Fletcher Henderson Orchestra	Walter Johnson	Savoy Ballroom, Harlem, NY
Mar. 7, 1937	Duke Ellington Orchestra	Sonny Greer	Savoy Ballroom, Harlem, NY
May 11, 1937	Benny Goodman Orchestra	Gene Krupa	Savoy Ballroom, Harlem, NY
Jun. 10, 1937	Noble Sissle Orchestra	Jack Carter	Memorial Hall, Dayton, OH
Nov. 15, 1937	Jimmy Dorsey Orchestra	Ray McKinley	Savoy Ballroom, Harlem, NY
Jan. 16, 1938	Count Basie Orchestra	'Papa' Jo Jones	Savoy Ballroom, Harlem, NY
Jul. 31,1938	Horace Henderson's CBS Band	Alvin Burroughs	Savoy Ballroom, Chicago, IL

CHICK WEBB DISCOGRAPHY

This discography is a compilation of the discography provided with ***THE COMPLETE CHICK WEBB & ELLA FITZGERALD DECCA SESSIONS*** (1934-1941) Mosaic Records CD 252-MD-CD and New Hot Discography by Charles Delauney, for all non-Decca sessions and to fill in some blanks. Editor's note, this discography includes only original USA first pressings and does not include foreign releases and/or releases of off-air broadcasts.

THE JUNGLE BAND: Ward Pinkett (tp, vo), Edwin Swayzee (tp), Robert Horton (tb), Hilton Jefferson, Louis Jordan (as), Elmer Williams (ts), Don Kirkpatrick (p), John Trueheart (bjo), Elmer James (tu), Chick Webb (d). NYC, June 14, 1929.
E30039 Dog Bottom (WP-vo) Br 4450

JUNGLE BAND: Same as above except the reeds double on clarinet and Trueheart switches to guitar. NYC, June 27, 1929.
E30091 Jungle Mama Br 4450

CHICK WEBB AND HIS ORCHESTRA: Shelton Hemphill, Louis Hunt (tp), Louis Bacon (tp, vo), Jimmy Harrison (tb), Benny Carter (cl, as, arr), Hilton Jefferson (cl, as), Elmer Williams (cl, ts), Don Kirkpatrick (p), John Trueheart (g), Elmer James (b), Chick Webb (d). NYC, March 30, 1931.
E36432 Heebie Jeebies Vo 1607
E36433 I'm Left With The Blues In My Heart (LB-vo) (BC-arr) Br 6156
E36434 Soft And Sweet Vo 1607

LOUIS ARMSTRONG WITH CHICK WEBB ORCHESTRA: Louis Armstrong, Louis Bacon, Louis Hunt, Billy Hicks (tp), Charlie Green (tb), Pete Clark, Edgar Sampson, Elmer Williams (s), Don Kirkpatrick (p), John Trueheart (g), Elmer James (b), Chick Webb (d). Camden, December 21, 1932.
74820 That's My Home (LA-vo) Vi 24200
75821 Hobo You Can't Ride This Train (LA-vo) Vi 24200
74822 I Hate To Leave You Now (LA-vo) Vi 24204
74823 You'll Wish You'd Never Been Born (LA-vo) Vi 24204 Mezz Mezzrow plays the bells.

CHICK WEBB AND HIS ORCHESTRA: Mario Bauza, Renald Jones, Taft Jordan (tp), Sandy Williams (tb), Pete Clark, Edgar Sampson, Elmer Williams (s), Joe Steele (p), John Trueheart (bjo, g), John Kirby (b), Chick Webb (d), Benny Carter (arr). NYC, December 20, 1933/15 Jan 1934.
152658 On The Sunny Side Of The Street (TJ-vo) Co2875D
152687 Get Together (BC-arr) Co2883D
152659 Darktown Strutters Ball Co2875D
152686 When Dreams Come True Co2883D

MEZZ MEZZROW AND HIS ORCHESTRA: Max Kaminsky, Renald Jones, Chelsea Qualey (tp), Floyd O'Brian (tb, arr), Mezz Mezzrow (cl, as, arr), Benny Carter (as), Bud Freeman (ts), Willie "The Lion" Smith (p), John Kirby (b), Chick Webb (d), Alex Hill (arr). NYC, May 7, 1934.
82393 Apologies Vi 25019
82394 Sendin' The Vipers Vi 25019
82392 Old Fashioned Love Vi 25202
82395 35th And Calumet Vi 25202

CHICK WEBB AND HIS ORCHESTRA: Mario Bauza, Renald Jones, Taft Jordan (tp), Sandy Williams (tb), Pete Clark, Edgar Sampson, Elmer Williams (s), Joe Steele (p), John Trueheart (bjo, g), John Kirby (b), Chick Webb (d), Van Alexander, Edgar Sampson (arr). NYC, May 9/15, 1934.
152733 I Can't Dance (TJ-vo) Co 2920D
152743 Imagination Co 2920D
152735 Why Should I Beg For Love (TJ-vo) Co 2926D
152740 Stomping At The Savoy Co 2926D

Bobby Stark (tp) replaces Jones, Wayman Carver (ts, f, arr), Fernando Arbello (tb) added. July 6, 1934.
152770 True OK 41571
152772 If It Ain't Love OK 41571
152679 Blue Minor OK 41572
152771 Lonesome Moments OK 41572

Claude Jones (tb) replaces Arbello. September 10, 1934.
38593 Rhythm Man (TJ-vo) (ES-arr) De 173
38594 On The Sunny Side Of The Street (TJ-vo) (ES-arr) De 172
38595 Lona (ES-arr) De 173
38596 Blue Minor (ES-arr) De 172

Same. November 19, 1934.
39138 It's Over Because We're Through (TJ-vo) (ES-arr) De 483
39140 Don't Be That Way (ES-arr) De 483
39141 What A Shuffle (ES-arr) De 1087
39142 Blue Lou (ES-arr) De 1065

Charles Linton (vo) Ella Fitzgerald (vo) added. June 12, 1935.
39615 Down Home Rag (WC-arr) De 785
39616 Are You Here To Stay? (CL-vo) (prob. ES-arr) De 494
39617 Love And Kisses (EF-vo) De 494

Bill Thomas (b) replaces Kirby. October 12, 1935.
60054 Rhythm And Romance (EF-vo) De 588
60055 Moonlight And Magnolias (EF-vo) De 588
60056 I'll Chase The Blues Away (EF-vo) (poss. ES-arr) De 640

60057 I May Be Wrong (But I Think You're Wonderful) (TJ-vo) De 64
60058 Facts And Figures (ES-arr) De 830

Same. April 7, 1936.
61000 Crying My Heart Out For You (EF-vo) (VA-arr) De 785
61001 Under The Spell Of the Blues (EF-vo)(prob.ES-arr) De 831
61002 When I Get Low, I Get High (EF-vo) (VA-arr) De 1123

Nat Story (tb) replaces Jones. June 2, 1936.
61123 Go Harlem (ES-arr) De 995
61124 Sing Me A Swing Song (And Let Me Dance) (EF-vo) (VA-arr) De 830
61125 A Little Bit Later On (EF-vo) (VA-arr) De 831
61126 Love, You're Just A Laugh (EF-vo) (VA-arr) De 1114
61127 Devoting My Time To You (EF-vo) (VA-arr) De 995

Mario Bauza, Bobby Stark, Taft Jordan (tp), Nat Story, Sandy Williams (tb), Pete Clark (cl, as), Edgar Sampson (as), Teddy McRae (ts), Wayman Carver (bs), Tommy Fulford (p), John Trueheart (g), Beverly Peer (b), Chick Webb (d), Ella Fitzgerald (vo), Van Alexander (arr). NYC, October 29, 1936.
61361 (If You Can't Sing It) You'll Have To Swing It (EF-vo) De 1032
61362 Swinging On The Reservation (EF-vo) (VA-arr) De 1065
61363 I Got The Spring Fever Blues (EF-vo) (VA-arr) De 1087
61364 Vote For Mr. Rhythm (EF-vo) (VA-arr) De 1032

ELLA FITZGERALD AND HER SAVOY EIGHT: Taft Jordan (tp), Sandy Williams (tb), Pete Clark (cl), Teddy McRae (ts), Tommy Fulford (p), John Trueheart (g), Beverly Peer (b), Chick Webb (d), Ella Fitzgerald (vo), Van Alexander (arr). NYC, November 18, 1936.
61419 My Last Affair (EF-vo) (VA-arr) De 1061
61420 Organ Grinder's Swing (EF-vo) (VA-arr) De 1062
61421 Shine (EF-vo) De 1062
61422 The Darktown Strutter's Ball (EF-vo) De 1061

CHICK WEBB AND HIS ORCHESTRA: Mario Bauza, Bobby Stark, Taft Jordan (tp), Nat Story, Sandy Williams (tb), Pete Clark (as), Louis Jordan (as, vo), Teddy McRae (ts), Wayman Carver (ts, bs), Tommy Fulford (p), John Trueheart (g), Beverly Peer (b), Chick Webb (d), Ella Fitzgerald, Charles Linton (vo), Van Alexander (arr). NYC, January 14/15, 1937.
61527 Oh Yes, Take Another Guess (EF-vo) (VA-arr) De 1123
61528 Love Marches On (CL-vo) (VA-arr) De 1115
61520 There's Frost On The Moon (EF, LJ, CL-vo) (VA-arr) De 1114
61530 Gee! But You're Swell (LJ-vo) (VA-arr) De 1115

JIMMY MUNDY & HIS SWING CLUB SEVEN: Walter Fuller (tp, vo), James Young (tb), Omer Simeon (as,cl), Jim Mundy (ts), Billy Kyle (p), Dick Palmer (g), Quinn Wilson (b). Chick Webb (d). NYC March 3, 1937.

M160 Ain't Misbehavin' (WF-vo) Va 598
M159 I Surrender Dear (WF-vo) Va 598

CHICK WEBB AND HIS ORCHESTRA: Mario Bauza, Bobby Stark, Taft Jordan (tp), Nat Story, Sandy Williams (tb), Pete Clark (as), Chauncey Haughton (s), Teddy McRae (ts), Wayman Carver (ts, bs), Tommy Fulford (p), John Trueheart (g), Beverly Peer (b), Chick Webb (d), Ella Fitzgerald, Charles Linton (vo), Louis Jordan (vo), Van Alexander, Charlie Dixon, Edgar Sampson (arr). NYC, March 24, 1937.
62064 Rusty Hinge (LJ-vo) (VA-arr) De 1273
62065 Wake Up And Live (EF, LJ, CL-vo) (VA-arr) De 1213
62066 It's Swell Of You (LJ-vo) (VA-arr) De 1213
62067 You Showed Me The Way (EF-vo) (VA-arr) De 1220
62068 Clap Hands! Here Comes Charley (ES-arr) De 1220
62069 Cryin' Mood (EF-vo) (VA-arr) De 1273
62072 Love Is The Thing, So They Say (EF-vo) (VA-arr) De 1356
62073 That Naughty Waltz (CD-arr) De 1356

THE GOTHAM STOMPERS: Cootie Williams (tp), Sandy Williams (tb), Barney Bigard (cl), Johnny Hodges (as), Harry Carney (bs), Tommy Fulford (p), Bernard Addison (g), Billy Taylor (b), Chick Webb (d), Ivie Anderson (vo), Van Alexander, Wayman Carver (arr). NYC, March 25, 1937.
M301 My Honey's Loving Arms Va 626
M302 Did Anyone Ever Tell You (WC-arr) Va 541
M303 Alabamy Home Va626
M304 Where Are You (WC-arr) Va 541

ELLA FITZGERALD AND HER SAVOY EIGHT: Taft Jordan (tp), Sandy Williams (tb), Louis Jordan (cl, as), Teddy McRae (ts), Tommy Fulford (p), Bobby Johnson (g), Beverly Peer (b), Chick Webb (d), Ella Fitzgerald (vo), Van Alexander (arr). NYC, May 24, 1937.
62213 All Over Nothing At All (EF-vo) (VA-arr) De 1339
62214 If You Ever Should Leave (EF-vo) (VA-arr) De 1302
62215 Everyone's Wrong But Me (EF-vo) De 1302
62216 Deep In The Heart Of The South (EF-vo) De 1339

CHICK WEBB AND HIS LITTLE CHICKS: Chauncey Haughton (cl), Wayman Carver (fl, arr), Tommy Fulford (p), Beverly Peer (b), Chick Webb (d). NYC, September 21/November 1, 1937.
62618 In A Little Spanish Town (WC-arr) De 1513
62619 I Got Rhythm (WC-arr) De 1759
62620 I Ain't Got Nobody (WC-arr) De 1513
62737 Sweet Sue, Just You (WC-arr) De 1759

CHICK WEBB AND HIS ORCHESTRA: Mario Bauza, Bobby Stark, Taft Jordan (tp), Nat Story, Sandy Williams (tb), Chauncey Haughton (cl, as), Louis Jordan (as), Teddy McRae, Wayman Carver (ts), Tommy Fulford (p), Bobby Johnson (g), Beverly Peer (b), Chick Webb (d), Ella Fitzgerald (vo), Van Alexander, Charlie Dixon (arr). NYC, October 27/November

1/2, 1937.
62725 Just A Simple Melody (EF-vo) (VA-arr) De 1521
62726 I Got A Guy (EF-vo) (VA-arr) De 1681
62727 Strictly Jive De 1586
62728 Holiday In Harlem (EF-vo) De 1521
62738 Rock It For Me (EF-vo) (VA-arr) De 1586
62739 Squeeze Me (CD-arr) De 1716
62740 Harlem Congo (CD-arr) De 1681

CHICK WEBB AND HIS ORCHESTRA: Mario Bauza, Bobby Stark, Taft Jordan (tp), Nat Story, Sandy Williams (tb), Garvin Bushell (cl, as), Louis Jordan (as), Teddy McRae (ts), Wayman Carver (ts, fl), Tommy Fulford (p), Bobby Johnson (g), Beverly Peer (b), Chick Webb (d), Ella Fitzgerald (vo), Van Alexander, Edgar Sampson (arr). NYC, December 17, 1937.
62886 I Want To Be Happy (EF-vo) (VA-arr) De 15039 (12")
62887 The Dipsy Doodle (EF-vo) (VA-arr) De 1587
62888 If Dreams Come True (EF-vo) (ES-arr) De 1716
62889 Hallelujah! (EF-vo) (VA-arr) De 15039 (12")
62890 Midnite In A Madhouse De 1587

ELLA FITZGERALD AND HER SAVOY EIGHT: Taft Jordan (tp), Sandy Williams (tb), Louis Jordan (cl, as), Teddy McRae (ts), Tommy Fulford (p), Bobby Johnson (g), Beverly Peer (b), Chick Webb (d), Ella Fitzgerald (vo), Van Alexander (arr). NYC, December 21, 1937.
62896 Bei Mir Bist Du Schon (Means That You're Grand) (EF-vo) (VA-arr) De 1596
62897 It's My Turn Now (EF-vo) De 1596

Same. January 25, 1938. 63225 It's Wonderful (EF-vo) De 1669
63226 I Was Doing All Right (EF-vo) (VA-arr) De 1669

CHICK WEBB AND HIS ORCHESTRA: Mario Bauza, Bobby Stark, Taft Jordan (tp), George Matthews, Nat Story, Sandy Williams (tb), Garvin Bushell (cl, as), Louis Jordan (as), Teddy McRae, Wayman Carver (ts, arr), Tommy Fulford (p), Bobby Johnson (g), Beverly Peer (b), Chick Webb (d), Ella Fitzgerald (vo), Van Alexander (arr). NYC, May 2, 1938.
63693 A-Tisket A-Tasket (EF, band-vo) (VA-arr) De 1840
63694 Heart Of Mine (EF-vo) De 2721
63695 I'm Just A Jitterbug (EF-vo) (VA-arr) De 1899
63696 Azure (VA-arr) De 1899
63707 Spinnin' The Webb (WC-arr) De 2021
63708 Liza (All The Clouds'll Roll Away) (VA-arr) De 1840

ELLA FITZGERALD AND HER SAVOY EIGHT: Taft Jordan (tp), Sandy Williams (tb), Louis Jordan (cl, as), Teddy McRae (ts), Tommy Fulford (p), Bobby Johnson (g), Beverly Peer (b), Chick Webb (d), Ella Fitzgerald (vo), Van Alexander (arr). NYC, May 3, 1938.
63703 This Time It's Real (EF-vo) De 1806
63704 (Oh! Oh!) What Do You Know About Love (EF-vo) De 1967
63705 You Can't Be Mine (AndSomeone Else's Too) (EF-vo) De 1806

63706 We Can't Go On This Way (EF-vo) De 1846
63709 (I've Been) Saving Myself For You (EF-vo) De 1846
63710 If You Only Knew (EF-vo) De 1967

CHICK WEBB AND HIS ORCHESTRA: Mario Bauza, Bobby Stark (tp), Taft Jordan (tp, vo), George Matthews, Nat Story, Sandy Williams (tb), Garvin Bushell (cl, as), Hilton Jefferson (as), Teddy McRae (ts), Wayman Carver (ts, bs), Tommy Fulford (p), Bobby Johnson (g), Beverly Peer (b), Chick Webb (d), Ella Fitzgerald (vo), Van Alexander (arr). NYC, June 9, 1938.
63934 Pack Up Your Sins And Go To The Devil (EF-vo) (VA-arr) De 1894
63935 MacPherson Is Rehearsin' (To Swing) (EF-vo) (VA-arr) De 2080
63936 Everybody Step (EF-vo) (VA-arr) De 1894
63937 Ella (EF, TJ-vo) (VA-arr) De 2148

Same. August 17, 1938.
64459 Wacky Dust (EF-vo) (VA-arr) De 2021
64460 Gotta Pebble In My Shoe (EF-vo) (VA-arr) De 2231
64461 I Can't Stop Loving You (EF-vo) (VA-arr) De 2310
64464 Who Ya Hunchin' De 2231
64465 I Let A Tear Fall In The River (EF-vo) (VA-arr) De 2080

ELLA FITZGERALD AND HER SAVOY EIGHT: Taft Jordan (tp), Sandy Williams (tb), Hilton Jefferson (as), Teddy McRae (ts), Tommy Fulford (p), Bobby Johnson (g), Beverly Peer (b), Chick Webb (d), Ella Fitzgerald (vo). NYC, August 18, 1938.
64462 Strictly From Dixie (EF-vo) De 2202
64463 Woe Is Me (EF-vo) De 2202

CHICK WEBB AND HIS ORCHESTRA: Dick Vance, Bobby Stark, Taft Jordan (tp), George Matthews, Nat Story, Sandy Williams (tb), Garvin Bushell (cl, as), Hilton Jefferson (as), Teddy McRae (ts), Wayman Carver (ts, arr), Tommy Fulford (p), Bobby Johnson (g), Beverly Peer (b), Chick Webb (d), Ella Fitzgerald (vo), Van Alexander (arr). NYC, October 6, 1938.
64573 F. D. R. Jones (EF-vo) (VA-arr) De 2105
64574 I Love Each Move You Make (EF-vo) (VA-arr) De 2105
64575 It's Foxy (EF-vo) (WC-arr) De 2309
64576 I Found My Yellow Basket (EF, band-vo) (VA-arr) De 2148

Same February 17, 1939.
65039 Undecided (EF-vo) (VA-arr) De 2323
65040 'Taint What You Do (It's The Way That Cha Do It) (EF-vo) De 2310
65041 In The Groove At The Grove De 2323
65042 One Side Of Me (EF-vo) De 2556
65043 My Heart Belongs To Daddy (EF-vo) (WC-arr) De 2309

John Trueheart (g) replaces Johnson. March 2/April 21, 1939
65094 Sugar Pie (EF-vo) De 2665

65095 It's Slumbertime Along The Swanee (EF-vo) De 2389
65096 I'm Up A Tree (EF-vo) De 2468
65097 Chew Chew Chew Chew (Your Bubble Gum) (EF, band-vo) De 2389
65445 Have Mercy (EF-vo) De 2468
65446 Little White Lies (EF-vo) De 2556
65447 Coochi-Coochi-Coo (EF-vo) De 2803
65448 That Was My Heart (EF-vo) De 2665

ELLA FITZGERALD AND HER SAVOY EIGHT: Taft Jordan (tp), Sandy Williams (tb), Hilton Jefferson (as), Teddy McRae (ts), Tommy Fulford (p), John Trueheart (g), Beverly Peer (b), Chick Webb (d), Ella Fitzgerald (vo). NYC, March 2, 1939.
65092 Once Is Enough For Me (EF-vo) De 2451
65093 I Had To Live And Learn (EF-vo) De 2581
65441 Don't Worry 'Bout Me (EF-vo) De 2451
65442 If Anything Happened To You (EF-vo) De 2481
65443 If That's What You're Thinking, You're Wrong (EF-vo) De 2581
65444 If You Ever Change Your Mind (EF-vo) De 2481

Label codes:
Br=Brunswick, Co=Columbia, De=Decca, OK=Okeh, Va=Variety, Vi=Victor, Vo=Vocalion.

Personnel codes:
arr=arranger, as=alto saxophone, b=bass, bjo=banjo, bs=baritone saxophone, cl=clarinet, d=drums, f=flute, g=guitar, p=piano, s=saxophone, tb=trombone, tp=trumpet, ts=tenor saxophone, tu=tuba, vo=vocal.

PHOTO/ILLUSTRATION CREDITS

Cover photo, © Centerstream Publications

Page 1, http://www.angelfire.com/mac/keepitlive/drummers/Webb/webb.htm

Page 4, http://www.soulwalking.co.uk/Ella%20Fitzgerald.html

Page 5, http://www.filmmusicsociety.org/news_events/features/2013/012913.html

Page 7, http://ghosttrainorchestra.com/?page=2

Page 8, http://www.savoyplaque.org/amstnews/1926/1926.htm

Page 9, http://www.longwharf.org/aint-misbehavin-hot-spots-harlem

Page 10, Top, http://leclownlyrique.wordpress.com/2011/02/18/8373/ Photo by Cornell Capa

Bottom, Left, http://photos.allaboutjazz.com/gallery_image.php?id=81584#.U4Tc5sKKDIU

Center, http://riverwalkjazz.stanford.edu/program/fletcher-henderson-and-don-redman-birth-big-band-reed-section songbook1.wordpress.

Right, http://www.redhotjazz.com/royalflush.html

Page 11, http://www.pinterest.com/pin/496803402615219013/

Page 12, Top, http://digital.1320records.com/search/release.php?release_id=603

Middle, http://www.pinterest.com/explore/jazz-club/ Lebreght Music & Arts/Corbis

Bottom, http://www.drumarchive.com/frankwolf/

Page 13, Top, Author's collection, April 1927 *Leedy Topics*

Middle, http://swingdjresources.com/chick-webb-dog-bottom/

Bottom, http://rpowell.livejournal.com/56357.html

Page 14, Top, Author's collection, *Gretsch Drums, The Legacy of "That Great Gretsch Sound"*

Bottom, http://jazzmostly.com/tag/harlem

Page 15, Left, http://www.drummerworld.com/drummers/Sonny_Greer.html

Right, http://songbook1.wordpress.com/pp/sw/composers-and-lyricists/cab-calloway/cab-calloway-minnie-the-moocher-and-other-early-songs-2/

Page 16, http://sirismm.si.edu/siris/top_images/acah.top.08_2009.htm Photo by Addison Scurlock, Smithsonian Images

Page 17, http://brushbeat.org/Articles.php Photo by Charles Peterson

Page 18, Top, http://www.yehoodi.com/comment/79178/anyone-track-down-the-lindy-hop-newspaper-cover/2

Middle, http://www.lindycircle.com/history/lindy_hop/

Bottom, http://www.lindycircle.com/history/lindy_hop/

Page 19, Top, http://bostonartsdiary.com/wordpress/2012/09/the-savoy-king-chick-webb-and-the-music-that-changed-america/

Middle, Author's collection, 1928 *Leedy Catalogue*

Bottom, http://www.downbeat.com/default.asp?sect=stories&subsect=story_detail&sid=1048

Page 20, Top, http://www.zazzle.com/savoy+gifts

Bottom, Author's collection, *Max On Swing*

Page 21, http://jazzarium.pl/przeczytaj/artyku%C5%82y/chick-webb-ojciec-nas-wszystkich-w-109-rocznic%C4%99-urodzin-legendarnego-drummera Frank Driggs Collection

Page 22, Top, http://themusicsover.com/2010/01/29/page/2/

Bottom, http://www.threeperfectminutes.com/2009/04/1931-part-2-blues-jive.html

Page 23, https://jazzlives.wordpress.com/tag/chick-webb/17

Page 24, Ron Middlebrook collection

Page 25, http://www.morethings.com/music/ella_fitzgerald/index.htm

Page 26, Top, http://www.blackpast.org/aah/apollo-theatre-1913 "Public Domain"

Bottom, http://dlmediamusic.com/artist/chick-webb-ella-fitzgerald/

Page 27, Top, http://www.tajmahalfoxtrot.com/?p=2541

Bottom, Author's collection, September 1937 *Metronome*

Page 28, http://dlmediamusic.com/artist/chick-webb-ella-fitzgerald/ Photograph by PoPsie.

Page 29, Author's collection, January 1938 *Metronome*

Page 30, Top, Author's collection, *Boy ten Hove's caricatures*

Bottom, Author's collection, Courtesy of *Eddie Condon's Scrapbook Of Jazz*, Galahad Books, New York

Page 31, http://jazzprofiles.blogspot.de/2009/05/davy-tough-1908-1948.html

Page 32, Top, http://forward.com/articles/107518/anything-you-can-do/ Getty Images

Bottom, http://leclownlyrique.wordpress.com/2011/02/18/8373/ Photo by Gjon Mili

Page 33, Top, http://museumsanfernandovalley.blogspot.de/2013/09/cherishing-our-valley-2013-font.html

Bottom, Author's collection, September 1937 *Metronome*

Page 34, Top, http://theharlemswingdancesociety.blogspot.de/2012/05/join-us-downtown-to-celebrate-chick.html

Bottom, http://www.rottentomatoes.com/celebrity/gene_krupa/pictures/

Page 35, Top, Left, http://www.drumlessons.com/drummers/pictures/chick-webb-pictures/

Right, http://www.drummerworld.com/drummers/Gene_Krupa.html

Bottom, http://theharlemswingdancesociety.blogspot.it/2012/12/save-date-janaury-16th-2013-75th.html

Page 36, Top, Dave Brown collection

Middle, Author's collection, October 1940 *Metronome*. Courtesy Fred Gretsch Enterprises, Ltd. photo archives

Bottom, Left, Author's collection, February 1938 *Metronome*

Right, http://www.mutanteggplant.com/vitro-nasu/2012/08/

Page 37, Top, Author's collection, February 1938 *Metronome*

Bottom, Author's collection, February 1938 *Metronome*

Page 38, Author's collection, 1939 Gretsch Catalogue. Courtesy Fred Gretsch Enterprises, Ltd. photo archives

Page 39, Author's collection, April 1939 *Metronome.* Courtesy Fred Gretsch Enterprises, Ltd. photo archives

Page 40, Top, http://rymimg.com/lk/f/l/e6692bca12f909b5978f96fdec153ce3/2942366.jpg

Bottom, Author's collection, September 1937 *Metronome*

Page 41, http://morgue.afro.com/AfroOmeka/exhibits/show/east-baltimore-memories/community-institutions/item/129

Page 42, Top, Author's collection, July 1938 *Metronome*

Bottom, http://www.drummerworld.com/drummers/Chick_Webb.html Institute of Jazz Studies, Rutgers University

Page 43, 1939, *Popular Mechanics.* Courtesy Fred Gretsch Enterprises, Ltd. photo archives

Page 44, Top, Dave Brown collection. Frank Driggs

Bottom, http://www.postercentral.com/newspapers.htm

Page 45, Top, http://www.corbisimages.com/stock-photo/rights-managed/U880420INP/chick-webb-mourners-outside-church Corbis Images

Bottom, https://www.wbgo.org/blog/you-dont-know-jazz-with-dr-lewis-porter-chick-webb

Page 46, Top, Photo by Judith Falzerano

Bottom, Photo by Judith Falzerano

Page 47, Top, http://www.drummerworld.com/drummers/Chick_Webb.html

Middle, Photo by Judith Falzerano

Bottom, Photo by Judith Falzerano

Page 48, Top, Author's collection, 1939 Gretsch Catalogue

Middle, Photo by Judith Falzerano

Bottom, http://theharlemswingdancesociety.blogspot.it/2012/05/join-us-downtown-to-celebrate-chick.html

Page 49, Top, http://www.musicfilmweb.com

Middle, http://www.drumarchive.com/frankwolf/

Bottom, Author's collection

Page 50, Author's collection

Page 51, Top, Photo by Judith Falzerano

Bottom, http://mediadiversified.org/2013/08/08/photo-gallery-jazz-artists-of-old snapshot-2013-08-07-23-39-46/

Page 52, Top, Photo by Judith Falzerano

Middle, Author's collection, *Boy ten Hove's caricatures*

Bottom Left, Photo by Chet Falzerano

Right, http://theharlemswingdancesociety.blogspot.it/2012/12/save-date-janaury-16th-2013-75th.html

Page 53, Top, http://www.amazon.com/Stompin-at-Savoy-Chick-Webb/dp/B00005UWTT/ref=nosim/?tag=chickenajourn-20

Bottom, Photo by Judith Falzerano

Page 54, Left/Right, Author's collection

Back Cover, Photo by Judith Falzerano

Available from:

Mosaic® RECORDS

http://www.mosaicrecords.com

Chick Webb & Ella Fitzgerald Decca Sessions (1934-41) (#252)

Mosaic Records Limited Edition Box Set

"If the old New Orleans drummers had given jazz its first pulse, it was Chick Webb who gave the music its first taste of raw, sovereign power from the drum chair. After years in the shadows, the drums suddenly pushed front and center with the big swing bands. But even before swing took the national stage, Webb had become the first great drummer-bandleader to saturate a spotlight with star power and charisma."
- John McDonough

Limited Edition: 5,000 copies
8 CDs - $136.00

More Great Books from Centerstream...

2-BASS HITS
Fundamentals of Playing 2-Bass Drums
by Dave "Bedrock" Bedrosian
This book/CD pack will help drum students learn: the fundamentals of playing two bass drums; important rhythms that all drummers should know; how to play confidently with both the feet and the hands; grooves in contemporary pop, rock & funk styles; and more.
00000247 Book/CD Pack.......................................$17.95

AFRO-CUBAN DRUMMING
by Glen Caruba
Glen Caruba is a talented percussionist who has worked with Bruce Springsteen, Sheryl Crow, Don Henley, Bruce Hornsby, Arturo Sandoval, and others. His comprehensive guide to traditional and contemporary styles of Afro-Cuban drumming will start the beginner out right and help professionals come up with new rhythms and ideas in this increasingly popular genre.
00000182 Book/CD Pack.......................................$19.95

MODERN PERCUSSION GROOVES
by Glen Caruba
Glen Caruba's first book, *Afro-Cuban Drumming,* touched on basic Latin percussion styles. This follow-up teaches how to incorporate these traditional rhythms and techniques into modern pop and rock playing. Covers instrument playing tips (congas, bongo, timbale, cowbell, shakers and more), funk grooves, pop ballads, Afro-Cuban 6/8, jazz-fusion grooves, cha-cha pop, and lots more. The CD features 40 tracks of examples.
00000228 Book/CD Pack.......................................$16.95

NEW DIRECTIONS AROUND THE DRUMS
by Mark Hamon
Endorsed by notables like Hal Blaine, Peter Erskine, Jim Chapin, and more, this book features a comprehensive, non-rudimental approach to the drumset for beginners to professionals! It combines straight drum-to-drum patterns with cross-sticking configurations, and includes open-ended free-style drum patterns for use as solos and fills.
00000170.......................................$14.95

SCHOOL OF HARD ROCKS
DVD
A Working Drummer's Guide to Real-World Drumming
by Bart Robley
Drummer, session man, teacher and Classic Drummer columnist Bart Robley has compiled the most essential rudiments that form the basis for all of his work. These exercises are not only great for beginners who need a solid foundation, but also perfect refreshers for intermediate to advanced players. By the time drummers are done with this book, their playing will come together into rhythms that can be used in a wide variety of playing situations.
00001203 ....$15.95
00001214 2-DVD Set $24.9 5

ASAP DRUM SET UP
INCLUDES TAB DVD
Learn Drum Set Up the Right Way
by Bart Robley
This excellent DVD teaches you how to put together, tune and set up your very first drums set. Drumming pro Bart Robley starts with the basics, covering in detail: opening the boxes, assembling the set, tuning, hardware, the drum rug, the bass drum, muffing and muting, ear plugs, set ups, teachers and lessons, and more! 1 hour, 10 minutes.
00001293 ....$10.99

DRUMMER'S SURVIVAL GUIDE
by Bart Robley
The perfect study companion for all drummers! With four of the most common ride patterns already written, in both one and two bar phrases, cuts transcription time in half. includes 40 essential rudiments, blank manuscript paper and more.!
00001331 Spiral-bound $12.99

ASAP RUDIMENTAL DRUMMING
DVD
by Bart Robley
In this instructional DVD, Telly Award winner, drummer, teacher & author, Bart Robley, teaches the basic rudiments that are essential for every drummer. Beginning with a solo based on paradiddles, Bart then breaks down the solo into its components. (Rudiment notation is displayed at the bottom of the screen.) Next, he demonstrates a paradiddle groove, and then introduces individual rudiments with the assistance of the Bart Robley Drum Club. Once assembled, the rudiments are used in a march titled, "The Red Panthers." Informative, fast-paced and fun - this DVD will set a solid foundation for your drumming career.... ASAP!!
00001332 ....$24.99

CENTERSTREAM

P.O. Box 17878 - Anaheim Hills, CA 92817
(714) 779-9390 www.centerstream-usa.com